THE BEST SMART QUOTES BOOK

WISDOM THAT CAN CHANGE YOUR LIFE

M. PREFONTAINE

Published by MP Publishing
Copyright © 2016

INTRODUCTION

What is it that makes a quote intelligent? What is it that makes any statement intelligent?

I would say that the essence of intelligence is that it changes a chaotic world into some sort of order. From a multitude of facts and events intelligence can see a line of commonality between different things and their interconnectedness.

An intelligent quote is simply one that expresses this intelligence in as succinct a fashion as possible.

Thoughts expressed succinctly have tremendous power. They can inspire and motivate, they can get a message across and they can provide insight.

This book provides over 1100 quotes from contributors ranging from Plato to Bob Dylan. There is a wide diversity of subject and viewpoints.

I hope this book will prove useful, interesting and that the quotes will resonate with you.

Most collectors collect tangibles. As a quotation collector, I collect wisdom, life, invisible beauty, souls alive in ink.
Terri Guillemets (1973 -)

CONTENTS

ARTS

Art is the elimination of the unnecessary.
Pablo Picasso (1881 – 1973)

The best way to have a good idea is to have lots of ideas.
Linus Pauling (1901 – 94)

If only we could pull out our brain and use only our eyes.
Pablo Picasso (1881 – 1973)

Art is never finished, only abandoned.
Leonardo da Vinci (1452 – 1519)

Every book, remember, is dead until a reader activates it by reading. Every time that you read you are walking among the dead, and, if you are listening, you just might hear prophecies.
Kathy Acker (1947 – 97)

The critic has to educate the public; the artist has to educate the critic.
Oscar Wilde (1854 – 1900)

Art struggles with chaos but it does so in order to render it sensory.
Gilles Deleuze (1925 – 95)

The aim of science is to make difficult things understandable in a simpler way; the aim of poetry is to state simple things in an incomprehensible way. The two are incompatible.
Paul Dirac (1902 – 84)

Art washes away from the soul the dust of everyday life.
Pablo Picasso (1881 – 1973)

I saw the angel in the marble and carved until I set him free.
Michelangelo (1475 – 1564)

Simplicity is the ultimate sophistication.
Leonardo da Vinci (1452 – 1519)

Art is a lie that makes us realize truth.
Pablo Picasso (1881 – 1973)

It took me four years to paint like Raphael, but a lifetime to paint like a child.
Pablo Picasso (1881 – 1973)

You can't use up creativity. The more you use, the more you have.
Maya Angelou (1928 – 2014)

We have art to save ourselves from the truth.
Friedrich Nietzsche (1844 – 1900)

Dancing is silent poetry.
Simonides (556 BC – 468 BC)

Sleep is an excellent way of listening to an opera.
James Stephens (1880 – 1950)

Painting is poetry that is seen rather than felt, and poetry is painting that is felt rather than seen.
Leonardo da Vinci (1452 – 1519)

Any fool can be happy. It takes a man with real heart to make beauty out of the stuff that makes us weep.
Clive Barker (1952 -)

Art is not what you see, but what you make others see.
Edgar Degas (1834 – 1917)

As far as I am concerned, a painting speaks for itself. What is the use of giving explanations, when all is said and done? A painter has only one language.
Pablo Picasso (1881 – 1973)

An artist is not paid for his labor but for his vision.
James McNeill Whistler (1834 – 1903)

Art is the imposing of a pattern on experience, and our aesthetic enjoyment is recognition of the pattern.
Alfred North Whitehead (1861 – 1947)

It is always fatal to have music or poetry interrupted.
George Eliot (1819 – 80)

Poetry: the best words in the best order.
Samuel Taylor Coleridge (1772 – 1834)

Never confuse the size of your paycheck with the size of your talent.
Marlon Brando (1924 – 2004)

We're not trying to entertain the critics ... I'll take my chances with the public.
Walt Disney (1901 – 66)

Art, like morality, consists of drawing the line somewhere.
GK Chesterton (1874 – 1936)

The enemy of art is the absence of limitations.
Orson Welles (1915 – 85)

Everywhere I go I find that a poet has been there before me.
Sigmund Freud (1856 – 1939)

BEAUTY

There is a road from the eye to the heart that does not go through the intellect.
GK Chesterton (1874 – 1936)

Perfection is achieved, not when there is nothing more to add, but when there is nothing left to take away.
Antoine de Saint-Exupéry (1900 – 44)

When I am working on a problem I never think about beauty. I only think about how to solve the problem. But when I have finished, if the solution is not beautiful, I know it is wrong.
Buckminster Fuller (1895 – 1983)

Beauty is no quality in things themselves: It exists merely in the mind which contemplates them; and each mind perceives a different beauty.
David Hume (1711 – 76)

It is amazing how complete is the delusion that beauty is goodness.
Leo Tolstoy (1828 – 1910)

Beauty is power; a smile is its sword.
John Ray (1627 – 1705)

A thing of beauty is a joy forever: its loveliness increases; it will never pass into nothingness.
John Keats (1795 – 1821)

Beauty is the wisdom of women. Wisdom is the beauty of men.
Chinese proverb

A bird doesn't sing because it has an answer, it sings because it has a song.
Maya Angelou (1928 – 2014)

Look at everything as though you were seeing it either for the first or last time.
Betty Smith (1896 – 1972)

You know you have achieved perfection in design, not when you have nothing more to add, but when you have nothing more to take away.
Antoine de Saint Exupery (1900 -44)

It is better to be beautiful than to be good, but it is better to be good than to be ugly.
Oscar Wilde (1854 – 1900)

Love of beauty is Taste. The creation of beauty is Art.
Ralph Waldo Emerson (1803 – 82)

Beauty is worse than wine; it intoxicates both the holder and the beholder.
Aldous Huxley (1894 – 1963)

Beauty isn't worth thinking about; what's important is your mind. You don't want a fifty-dollar haircut on a fifty-cent head.
Garrison Keillor (1942 -)

Beauty without grace is the hook without the bait.
Ralph Waldo Emerson (1803 – 82)

The innocent and the beautiful have no enemy but time.
William Butler Yeats (1865 – 1939)

Since love grows within you, so beauty grows. For love is the beauty of the soul.

Augustine of Hippo (354 - 430)

BUSINESS

Under capitalism, man exploits man. Under communism, it's just the opposite.
John Kenneth Galbraith (1908 – 2006)

You can't build a reputation on what you are going to do.
Henry Ford (1863 – 1947)

In the business world, everyone is paid in two coins: cash and experience. Take the experience first; the cash will come later.
Harold Geneen (1910 – 97)

In any great organization it is far, far safer to be wrong with the majority than to be right alone.
John Kenneth Galbraith (1908 – 2006)

Advertising is 85% confusion and 15% commission.
Fred Allen (1894 – 1956)

A good decision is based on knowledge and not on numbers.
Plato (428 BC – 347 BC)

When the capital development of a country becomes a by-product of the activities of a casino, the job is likely to be ill-done.
John Maynard Keynes (1883 – 1946)

As we look ahead into the next century, leaders will be those who empower others.
Bill Gates (1955 -)

It is not the employer who pays the wages. Employers only handle the money. It is the customer who pays the wages.
Henry Ford (1863 – 1947)

Entrepreneurs are simply those who understand that there is little difference between obstacle and opportunity and are able to turn both to their advantage.
Niccolo Machiavelli (1469 – 1527)

The hardest part about being an entrepreneur is that you will fail ten times for every success.
Adam Horwitz (1992 -)

An organization's ability to learn, and translate that learning into action rapidly, is the ultimate competitive advantage.
Jack Welch (1935 -)

Almost all quality improvement comes via simplification of design, manufacturing... layout, processes, and procedures.
Tom Peters (1942 -)

A bargain is something you don't need at a price you can't resist.
Franklin Jones (1879 – 1967)

Be fearful when others are greedy. Be greedy when others are fearful.
Warren Buffett (1930 -)

You can fool all the people all the time if the advertising is right and the budget is big enough.
Joseph E. Levine (1905 -87)

Whenever you see a successful business, someone once made a courageous decision.
Peter F Drucker (1909 – 2005)

Opportunities multiply as they are seized.
Sun Tzu (? - 496 BC)

The way to make money is to buy when blood is running in the streets.
John D Rockefeller (1839 - 1937)

Only when the tide goes out do you discover who's been swimming naked.
Warren Buffet (1932 -)

Vision without execution is just hallucination.
Henry Ford (1863 – 1947)

I was seldom able to see an opportunity until it had ceased to be one.
Mark Twain (1835 -1910)

The greatest ability in business is to get along with others and to influence their actions.
John Hancock (1737 – 93)

The superior man understands what is right; the inferior man understands what will sell.
Confucius (551 BC – 479 BC)

Price is what you pay. Value is what you get.
Warren Buffett (1930 -)

There is a tide in the affairs of men which, taken at the flood, leads on to fortune;
William Shakespeare (1564 – 1616)

The secret of getting ahead is getting started. The secret of getting started is breaking your complex, overwhelming tasks into small, manageable tasks, and then starting on the first one.
Mark Twain (1835 – 1910)

People don't buy for logical reasons. They buy for emotional reasons.
Zig Ziglar (1928 - 2012)

It is easier to build strong children than to repair broken men.
Frederick Douglass (1818 -95)

Let us remember: One book, one pen, one child, and one teacher can change the world.
Malala Yousafzai (1997 -)

It's the greatest poverty to decide that a child must die so that you may live as you wish.
Mother Teresa (1910 – 97)

Children, I suppose, are always unfinished business: they begin as part of your own body, and continue as separate as another continent.
Jeanette Winterson (1959 -)

Children find everything in nothing; men find nothing in everything.
Giacomo Leopardi (1798 – 1837)

Childhood is measured out by sounds and smells and sights, before the dark hour of reason grows.
John Betjeman (1906 – 84)

There is always one moment in childhood when the door opens and lets the future in.
Graham Greene (1904 – 91)

The world knows how to straighten out a spoiled child but never makes it up to a child deprived.
Robert Brault (1963 -)

Old age lives minutes slowly, hours quickly; childhood chews hours and swallows minutes.
Malcolm de Chazal (1902 – 81)

CHILDREN

Children are the living messages we send to a time we will not see.
John W. Whitehead (1948 -)

Don't worry that children never listen to you; worry that they are always watching you.
Robert Fulghum (1937 -)

The children now love luxury. They have bad manners, contempt for authority; they show disrespect for elders and love chatter in place of exercise.
Socrates (470 BC - 399 BC)

Youth would be an ideal state if it came a little later in life.
Herbert Asquith (1852 – 1928)

Age is foolish and forgetful when it underestimates youth.
JK Rowling (1965 -)

A baby is God's opinion that life should go on.
Carl Sandburg (1878 – 1967)

Insanity is hereditary. You get it from your children.
Sam Levenson (1911 – 80)

With kids, the days are long, but the years are short.
John Leguizamo (1964 -)

Adolescence is when children start trying to bring up their parents.
Richard Armour (1906 – 89)

The soul is healed by being with children.
Fyodor Dostoyevsky (1821 – 81)

If there must be trouble, let it be in my day, that my child may have peace.
Thomas Paine (1737 – 1809)

I think, at a child's birth, if a mother could ask a fairy godmother to endow it with the most useful gift, that gift should be curiosity.
Eleanor Roosevelt (1884 – 1962)

I'm not young enough to know everything.
J.M. Barrie (1860- 1937)

Delusions are often functional. A mother's opinions about her children's beauty, intelligence, goodness, et cetera ad nauseam, keep her from drowning them at birth.
Robert A. Heinlein (1907 – 88)

COURAGE

When you're at the end of your rope, tie a knot and hold on.
Theodore Roosevelt (1858 – 1918)

Courage is the price that life extracts for granting peace.
Amelia Earhart (1897 – 1937)

Be kind, for everyone you meet is fighting a harder battle.
Plato (428 BC – 348 BC)

In the depth of winter, I finally learned that within me there lay an invincible summer.
Albert Camus (1913 – 60)

The only thing that I have done that is not mitigated by luck, diminished by good fortune, is that I persisted, and other people gave up.
Harrison Ford (1942 -)

You may not control all the events that happen to you, but you can decide not to be reduced by them.
Maya Angelou (1928 – 2014)

Fear regret more than failure.
Taryn Rose

Courage is contagious. When a brave man takes a stand, the spines of others are stiffened.
Billy Graham (1918 -)

Courage is almost a contradiction in terms. It means a strong desire to live taking on the form of a readiness to die.
GK Chesterton (1874 – 1936)

Courage is as often the outcome of despair as of hope; in the one case we have nothing to lose, in the other, everything to gain.
Diane de Pointiers (1499 – 1566)

Cowardice, as distinguished from panic, is almost always simply a lack of ability to suspend the functioning of the imagination.
Ernest Hemingway (1899 – 1961)

Some have been thought brave because they were afraid to run away.
Thomas Fuller (1608 -61)

A ship is safe in harbor, but that is not what ships are for.
William GT Shedd (1820 -94)

The paradox of courage is that a man must be a little careless of his life in order to keep it.
GK Chesterton (1874 – 1936)

Man cannot discover new oceans unless he has the courage to lose sight of the shore.
Andre Gide (1869 – 1951)

The secret of happiness is freedom. The secret of freedom is courage.
Thucydides (460 BC – 390 BC)

When will you understand that being normal isn't necessarily a virtue? It rather denotes a lack of courage.
Alice Hoffman (1952 -)

DEATH

We all pay for life with death, so everything in between should be free.
Bill Hicks (1961 – 94)

The real question of life after death isn't whether or not it exists, but even if it does what problem this really solves.
Ludwig Wittgenstein (1889 – 1951)

Death may be the greatest of all human blessings.
Socrates (470 BC – 399 BC)

Death solves all problems - no man, no problem.
Joseph Stalin (1878 – 1953)

The great business of life is to be, to do, to do without, and to depart.
John, Viscount Morley (1838 – 1923)

Remembering that you are going to die is the best way I know to avoid the trap of thinking you have something to lose. You are already naked. There is no reason not to follow your heart.
Steve Jobs (1955 – 2011)

They say you die twice. One time when you stop breathing and a second time, a bit later on, when somebody says your name for the last time.
Banksy (1974 -)

Freedom for the wolves has often meant death to the sheep.
Isaiah Berlin (1909 – 97)

There are perhaps many causes worth dying for, but to me, certainly, there are none worth killing for.
Albert Dietrich (1829 – 1909)

Every man is born as many men and dies as a single one.
Martin Heidegger (1889 – 1976)

A doctor can bury his mistakes but an architect can only advise his clients to plant vines.
Frank Lloyd Wright (1868-1959)

I'd hate to die twice. It's so boring.
Richard Feynman (1918 – 88)

Every man's life ends the same way. It is only the details of how he lived and how he died that distinguish one man from another.
Ernest Hemmingway (1899 – 1961)

Death must be so beautiful. To lie in the soft brown earth, with the grasses waving above one's head, and listen to silence. To have no yesterday, and no to-morrow. To forget time, to forgive life, to be at peace.
Oscar Wilde (1854-1900)

Life is not lost by dying; life is lost minute by minute, day by dragging day, in all the thousand small uncaring ways.
Stephen Vincent Benet (1898-1943)

Death is a friend of ours; and he that is not ready to entertain him is not at home.
Francis Bacon (1561-1626)

The price of anything is the amount of life you exchange for it.
Henry David Thoreau (1817 - 62)

All men are cremated equal.
Spike Milligan (1918 – 2002)

ECONOMICS

One of the greatest pieces of economic wisdom is to know what you do not know.
John Kenneth Galbraith (1908 – 2006)

Economics is extremely useful as a form of employment for economists.
John Kenneth Galbraith (1908 – 2006)

The avoidance of taxes is the only intellectual pursuit that carries any reward.
John Maynard Keynes (1883 – 1946)

Plan beats no plan.
Tim Geithner (1961 -)

There is nothing to fear but fear itself.
Franklin D. Roosevelt (1882 – 1945)

Freedom in capitalist society always remains about the same as it was in ancient Greek republics: Freedom for slave owners.
Vladimir Ilyich Lenin (1870 – 1924)

Economics was like psychology, a pseudoscience trying to hide that fact with intense theoretical hyperelaboration.
Kim Stanley Robinson (1952 -)

The first lesson of economics is scarcity: There is never enough of anything to satisfy all those who want it. The first lesson of politics is to disregard the first lesson of economics.
Thomas Sowell (1930 -)

Economic statistics are like a bikini, what they reveal is important, what they conceal is vital.
Professor Sir Frank Holmes (1924 – 2011)

An economist is someone who, when he finds something that works in practice, tries to make it work in theory.
Walter Heller (1915 – 87)

If an exchange between two parties is voluntary, it will not take place unless both believe they will benefit from it. Most economic fallacies derive from the neglect of this simple insight, from the tendency to assume that there is a fixed pie that one party can only gain at the expense of another.
Milton Friedman (1912 – 2006)

An economist is a man who states the obvious in terms of the incomprehensible.
Alfred A. Knopf (1892 – 1984)

There ain't no such thing as a free lunch.
Robert A. Heinlein (1907 – 88)

There can be no real individual freedom in the presence of economic insecurity.
Chester Bowles (1901 - 1986)

An economist is an expert who will know tomorrow why the things he predicted yesterday didn't happen today.
Laurence J. Peter (1919 - 1988)

EDUCATION

You educate a man; you educate a man. You educate a woman; you educate a generation.
Brigham Young (1801 – 77)

Education: the inculcation of the incomprehensible into the indifferent by the incompetent.
John Maynard Keynes (1883 – 1946)

Education is teaching our children to desire the right things.
Plato (428 BC – 348 BC)

It is the mark of an educated mind to be able to entertain a thought without accepting it.
Aristotle (384 BC – 322 BC)

I cannot teach anybody anything. I can only make them think.
Socrates (470 BC – 399 BC)

If a man empties his purse into his head, no man can take it away from him. An investment in knowledge always pays the best interest.
Benjamin Franklin (1706 -90)

Nature has always had more power than education.
Voltaire (1694 – 1778)

A learned man is an idler who kills time by study.
George Bernard Shaw (1856 – 1950)

Imagine a school with children that can read or write, but with teachers who cannot, and you have a metaphor of the Information Age in which we live.
Peter Cochrane (1950 -)

Wit is educated insolence.
Aristotle (384 BC – 322 BC)

Education is a system of imposed ignorance.
Noam Chomsky (1928 -)

Education is not preparation for life; education is life itself.
John Dewey (1859 – 1952)

Education is not the filling of a bucket, but the lighting of a fire.
William Butler Yeats (1865-1939)

There are two kinds of teachers: the kind that fill you with so much quail shot that you can't move, and the kind that just gives you a little prod behind and you jump to the skies.
Robert Frost (1874 – 1963)

Education is what remains after one has forgotten what one has learned in school.
Albert Einstein (1879 - 1955)

Tell me and I forget. Teach me and I remember. Involve me and I learn.
Benjamin Franklin (1706 -90)

Education is our passport to the future, for tomorrow belongs to the people who prepare for it today.
Malcolm X (1925 -65)

It is impossible for a man to learn what he thinks he already knows.
Epictetus (55 – 135)

It is always a much easier task to educate uneducated people than to re-educate the mis-educated.

Herbert M. Shelton (1895 – 1985)

The difference between school and life? In school, you're taught a lesson and then given a test. In life, you're given a test that teaches you a lesson.

Tom Bodett (1955 -)

Real education must ultimately be limited to men who insist on knowing, the rest is mere sheep-herding.

Ezra Pound (1885 – 1972)

When one teaches, two learn.

Robert A. Heinlein (1907 – 88)

Education is learning what you didn't even know you didn't know.

Daniel J. Boorstin (1914 – 2004)

The only thing more expensive than education is ignorance.

Benjamin Franklin (1706 – 90)

Never seem more learned than the people you are with. Wear your learning like a pocket watch and keep it hidden. Do not pull it out to count the hours, but give the time when you are asked.

Lord Chesterfield (1694 – 1773)

Education is a vaccine for violence.

Edward James Olmos (1947 -)

When you educate a man you educate an individual when you educate a woman you educate a whole family.

Johnetta Cole (1936 -)

Education is an ornament in prosperity and a refuge in adversity.
Aristotle (384 BC – 322 BC)

There is no education like adversity.
Benjamin Disraeli (1804 – 81)

The task of the modern educator is not to cut down jungles but to irrigate deserts.
C.S. Lewis (1898 – 1963)

Learning isn't a means to an end; it is an end in itself.
Robert A. Heinlein (1907 – 88)

Natural abilities are like natural plants; they need pruning by study.
Francis Bacon (1561-1626)

ENVIRONMENT

Earth provides enough to satisfy every man's needs, but not every man's greed.
Mahatma Gandhi (1869 – 1948)

We do not inherit the earth from our ancestors; we borrow it from our children.
Native American Proverb

There are no passengers on Spaceship Earth. We are all crew.
Marshall McLuhan (1911 – 80)

The earth has a skin and that skin has diseases; one of its diseases is called man.
Friedrich Nietzsche (1844 – 1900)

The ultimate test of man's conscience may be his willingness to sacrifice something today for future generations whose words of thanks will not be heard.
Gaylord Nelson (1916 – 2005)

When one tugs at a single thing in nature, he finds it attached to the rest of the world.
John Muir (1838 – 1914)

In nature, nothing exists alone.
Rachel Carson (1907-1964)

Think globally, act locally.
Paul McCartney (1942 -)

You cannot affirm the power plant and condemn the smokestack, or affirm the smoke and condemn the cough.
Wendell Berry (1934 -)

One touch of nature makes the whole world kin.
William Shakespeare (1564-1616)

When the well's dry, we know the worth of water.
Benjamin Franklin (1706-1790)

Who are we? We find that we live on an insignificant planet of a humdrum star lost in a galaxy tucked away in some forgotten corner of a universe in which there are far more galaxies than people.
Carl Sagan (1934-1996)

We are living on this planet as if we had another one to go to.
Terri Swearingen (1956 -)

One planet, one experiment.
Edward O. Wilson (1929 -)

I conceive that the land belongs to a vast family of which many are dead, few are living, and countless numbers are still unborn.
Anon

If trees could scream, would we be so cavalier about cutting them down.
Jack Handey (1949 -)

It was not until we saw the picture of the earth, from the moon, that we realized how small and how helpless this planet is - something that we must hold in our arms and care for.
Margaret Mead (1901 -78)

Only to the white man was nature a 'wilderness'.
Luther Standing Bear (1868 – 1939)

Human history becomes more and more a race between education and catastrophe.
HG Wells (1866 – 1946)

The end of the human race will be that it will eventually die of civilization.
Ralph Waldo Emerson (1803 – 82)

In America today you can murder land for private profit. You can leave the corpse for all to see, and nobody calls the cops.
Paul Brooks (1959 -)

The universe is not required to be in perfect harmony with human ambition.
Carl Sagan (1934-1996)

Waste is a tax on the whole people.
Albert W. Atwood (1911 -75)

In nature there are neither rewards nor punishments; there are consequences.
Robert Green Ingersoll (1833 – 99)

Autumn is a second spring when every leaf is a flower.
Albert Camus (1913 -60)

Why should I care about future generations? What have they ever done for me?
Groucho Marx (1890 – 1977)

You are what what you eat eats.
Michael Pollan (1955 -)

In wine there is wisdom, in beer there is freedom, in water there is bacteria.

Benjamin Franklin (1706 -90)

FRIENDSHIP

A friend is one who has the same enemies as you have.
Abraham Lincoln (1809 – 65)

Fish and visitors smell in three days.
Benjamin Franklin (1706 -90)

A false friend and a shadow attend only while the sun shines.
Benjamin Franklin (1706 -90)

No man can be called friendless when he has God and the companionship of good books.
Elizabeth Barrett Browning (1806 – 61)

Everyone you will ever meet knows something you don't.
Bill Nye (1955 -)

Love is friendship set on fire.
Jeremy Taylor (1613 – 67)

Friendship ... is born at the moment when one man says to another "What! You too? I thought that no one but myself..."
C.S. Lewis (1898 – 1963)

The meeting of two personalities is like the contact of two chemical substances: if there is any reaction, both are transformed.
C.G. Jung (1875 – 1961)

The Internet is becoming the town square for the global village of tomorrow.
Bill Gates (1955 -)

Tact is the ability to describe others as they see themselves.
Abraham Lincoln (1809 - 65)

Somebody is sitting in the shade today because someone planted a tree a long time ago.
Warren Buffet (1932 -)

A single act of kindness throws out roots in all directions, and the roots spring up and make new trees.
Amelia Earhart (1897 – 1937)

If you go looking for a friend, you're going to find they're scarce. If you go out to be a friend, you'll find them everywhere.
Zig Ziglar (1928 - 2012)

What is a friend? A single soul dwelling in two bodies.
Aristotle (384 BC - 322 BC)

The best listeners listen between the lines.
Nina Malkin

Tact is the knack of making a point without making an enemy.
Isaac Newton (1643 – 1727)

We're born alone, we live alone, we die alone. Only through our love and friendship can we create the illusion for the moment that we're not alone.
Orson Welles (1915 – 85)

Friendship improves happiness, and abates misery, by doubling our joys, and dividing our grief.
Marcus Tullius Cicero (106 BC – 43 BC)

GOVERNMENT

Capitalism is the astounding belief that the most wickedest of men will do the most wickedest of things for the greatest good of everyone.
John Maynard Keynes (1883 – 1946)

You campaign in poetry. You govern in prose.
Mario Cuomo (1932 -)

Every election is a sort of advance auction sale of stolen goods.
H. L. Mencken (1880 - 1956)

As government expands liberty contracts.
Ronald Reagan (1911 – 2004)

Good people do not need laws to tell them to act responsibly, while bad people will find a way around the laws.
Plato (428 BC – 348 BC)

The heaviest penalty for declining to rule is to be ruled by someone inferior to yourself.
Plato (428 BC – 348 BC)

The best government is a benevolent tyranny tempered by an occasional assassination.
Voltaire (1694 – 1778)

Information is the currency of democracy.
Thomas Jefferson (1743 – 1826)

It is true that liberty is precious - so precious that it must be rationed.
Vladimir Lenin (1870 – 1924)

Bureaucracy is a giant mechanism operated by pygmies.
Balzac (1799 – 1850)

One man with a gun can control 100 without one.
Vladimir Lenin (1870 – 1924)

It is better to be feared than loved, if you cannot be both.
Niccolo Machiavelli (1469 – 1527)

It is enough that the people know there was an election. The people who cast the votes decide nothing. The people who count the votes decide everything.
Joseph Stalin (1878 – 1953)

What do I think of Western civilization? I think it would be a very good idea.
Mahatma Gandhi (1869 – 1948)

Government can't give us anything without depriving us of something else.
Henry Hazlitt (1894 – 1993)

If we don't believe in freedom of expression for people we despise, we don't believe in it at all.
Noam Chomsky (1928 -)

Civil government, so far as it is instituted for the security of property, is in reality instituted for the defense of the rich against the poor, or of those who have some property against those who have none at all.
Adam Smith (1723 – 90)

The worst government is the most moral. One composed of cynics is often very tolerant and humane. But when fanatics are on top there is no limit to oppression.
Henry Louis Mencken (1880 – 1956)

The oppressed are allowed once every few years to decide which particular representatives of the oppressing class are to represent and repress them.
Karl Marx (1818 – 83)

A government is the most dangerous threat to man's rights: it holds a legal monopoly on the use of physical force against legally disarmed victims.
Ayn Rand (1905 – 82)

The Constitution is not an instrument for the government to restrain the people, it is an instrument for the people to restrain the government - lest it come to dominate our lives and interests.
Patrick Henry (1736 – 99)

Government is not reason, it is not eloquence, it is force; like fire, a troublesome servant and a fearful master. Never for a moment should it be left to irresponsible action.
George Washington (1732 – 99)

Government's view of the economy could be summed up in a few short phrases: If it moves, tax it. If it keeps moving, regulate it. And if it stops moving, subsidise it.
Ronald Reagan (1911 – 2004)

In Italy for thirty years under the Borgias they had warfare, terror, murder and bloodshed but they produced Michelangelo, Leonardo da Vinci and the Renaissance. In Switzerland, they had brotherly love; they had five hundred

years of democracy and peace and what did they produce? The cuckoo clock.
Orson Welles (1915-85)

A nation of sheep will beget a government of wolves.
Edward R. Murrow (1908 -65)

A conservative is a man who believes that nothing should be done for the first time.
Alfred E. Wiggam (1871 – 1957)

HAPPINESS

Happiness equals reality minus expectations.
Tom Magliozzi (1937 – 2014)

The reason people find it so hard to be happy is that they always see the past better than it was, the present worse than it is, and the future less resolved than it will be.
Marcel Pagnol (1895 – 1974)

They say a person needs just three things to be truly happy in this world: someone to love, something to do, and something to hope for.
Tom Bodett (1955 -)

The secret of happiness, you see, is not found in seeking more, but in developing the capacity to enjoy less.
Socrates (470 BC – 399 BC)

Happiness is not a goal; it is a by-product.
Eleanor Roosevelt (1884 – 1962)

No man chooses evil because it is evil; he only mistakes it for happiness, the good he seeks.
Mary Wollstonecraft Shelley (1797 – 1851)

Happiness is a perfume you cannot pour on others without getting a few drops on yourself.
Ralph Waldo Emerson (1803 – 1882)

Happiness is beneficial for the body, but it is grief that develops the powers of the mind.
Marcel Proust (1871 – 1922)

Blessed is the man who, having nothing to say, abstains from giving us wordy evidence of the fact.
George Eliot (1819 – 80)

If you don't like something, change it. If you can't change it, change your attitude.
Maya Angelou (1928 – 2014)

Happiness is the only good. The time to be happy is now. The place to be happy is here. The way to be happy is to make others so.
Robert Green Ingersoll (1833 – 99)

Remember that failure is an event, not a person.
Zig Ziglar (1928 - 2012)

Doing what you like is freedom. Liking what you do is happiness.
Frank Tyger (1929 -)

Remember that happiness is a way of travel -- not a destination.
Agnes Repplier (1858 – 1950)

It was only a sunny smile, and little it cost in the giving, but like morning light it scattered the night and made the day worth living.
F. Scott Fitzgerald (1896 – 1940)

Let fear be a counselor and not a jailer.
Anthony Robbins (1960 -)

There are two ways of being happy: We must either diminish our wants or augment our means - either may do - the result is

the same and it is for each man to decide for himself and to do that which happens to be easier.

Benjamin Franklin (1706 -90)

All good things must come to an end, but all bad things can continue forever.

Thornton Wilder (1897 – 1975)

Happiness is the china shop; love is the bull.

H. L. Mencken (1880 - 1956)

Here's to alcohol, the rose colored glasses of life.

F. Scott Fitzgerald (1896 – 1940)

Don't let your happiness depend on something you may lose.

C.S. Lewis (1898 – 1963)

HOPE

Man can live about forty days without food, about three days without water, about eight minutes without air, but only for one second without hope.
Hal Lindsay (1929 -)

Hope is the feeling that the feeling you have isn't permanent.
Jean Kerr (1923 – 2003)

I don't think of all the misery, but of the beauty that still remains.
Anne Frank (1929 – 45)

Hope is a good breakfast, but it is a bad supper.
Francis Bacon (1561 – 1626)

There is a crack in everything.
That's how the light gets in.
Leonard Cohen (1934 -)

The road that is built in hope is more pleasant to the traveler than the road built in despair, even though they both lead to the same destination.
Marion Zimmer Bradley (1930 – 99)

Shoot for the moon, even if you fail, you'll land among the stars.
Cecelia Ahern (1981 -)

One lives in the hope of becoming a memory.
Antonio Porchia (1885 – 1968)

Hope never abandons you; you abandon it.
George Weinberg (1935 -)

Hope is the only universal liar who never loses his reputation for veracity.
Robert G Ingersoll (1833 - 99)

Hope deceives more men than cunning does.
Luc de Clapiers (1715 – 47)

Never deprive someone of hope — it may be all they have.
H Jackson Brown Jr (1940 -)

Hope and fear are inseparable. There is no hope without fear, nor any fear without hope.
François de la Rochefoucauld (1613 – 80)

Carve a tunnel of hope through the dark mountain of disappointment.
Martin Luther King, Jr. (1929 – 68)

Learn from yesterday, live for today, hope for tomorrow.
Albert Einstein (1879 – 1955)

The future is already here – it's just not evenly distributed.
William Gibson (1948 -)

It's never too late to be what you might have been.
George Eliot (1819 – 80)

Hope is faith holding out its hand in the dark.
George Iles (1960 -)

Hope is the thing with feathers, that perches in the soul, and sings the tune without words, and never stops at all.
Emily Dickinson (1830 – 86)

Hope costs nothing.
Sidonie Gabrielle (1873 – 1974)

Hope has two beautiful daughters. Their names are anger and courage; anger at the way things are, and courage to see that they do not remain the way they are.
Augustine of Hippo (354 -430)

Hope unbelieved is always considered nonsense. But hope believed is history in the process of being changed.
Jim Wallis (1948 -)

Hope is the only bee that makes honey without flowers.
Robert Green Ingersoll (1833 – 99)

To be truly radical is to make hope possible rather than despair convincing.
Raymond Williams (1921 – 88)

When you put faith, hope and love together, you can raise positive kids in a negative world.
Zig Ziglar (1926 – 2012)

Youth is easily deceived, because it is quick to hope.
Aristotle (384 BC – 322 BC)

Hope is like the sun, which, as we journey toward it, casts the shadow of our burden behind us.
Samuel Smiles (1812 – 1904)

Hope is the only good that is common to all men; those who have nothing else possess hope still.
Thales of Miletus (624 BC – 546 BC)

Hope is the companion of power, and mother of success; for who so hopes strongly has within him the gift of miracles.
Samuel Smiles (1812 – 1904)

Hope is the poor man's bread.
Thales of Miletus (624 BC – 546 BC)

The great French Marshall Lyautey once asked his gardener to plant a tree. The gardener objected that the tree was slow growing and would not reach maturity for 100 years. The Marshall replied, 'In that case, there is no time to lose; plant it this afternoon.
John Fitzgerald Kennedy (1917 – 63)

We set sail on this new sea because there is knowledge to be gained.
John Fitzgerald Kennedy (1917 – 63)

They are ill discoverers that think there is no land, when they can see nothing but sea.
Francis Bacon (1561-1626)

Hope is such a bait, it covers any hook.
Oliver Goldsmith (1728 – 74)

HUMAN NATURE

Common sense is the collection of prejudices acquired by age eighteen.
Albert Einstein (1879 - 1955)

Fashion is what you adopt when you don't know who you are.
Quentin Crisp (1908 – 99)

He that is good for making excuses is seldom good for anything else.
Benjamin Franklin (1706 -90)

Never apologize for showing feeling. When you do so, you apologize for the truth.
Benjamin Disraeli (1804 – 81)

We are all born ignorant, but one must work hard to remain stupid.
Benjamin Franklin (1706 -90)

Confidence is what you have before you understand the problem.
Woody Allen (1935 -)

An autobiography usually reveals nothing bad about its writer except his memory.
Benjamin Franklin (1706 -90)

The greatest monarch on the proudest throne is obliged to sit upon his own arse.
Benjamin Franklin (1706 -90)

Nearly all men can stand adversity, but if you want to test a man's character, give him power.
Abraham Lincoln (1809 – 65)

The mind is like an iceberg; it floats with one-seventh of its bulk above water.
Sigmund Freud (1856 – 1939)

Nothing is more fairly distributed than common sense: no one thinks he needs more of it than he already has.
Rene Descartes (1596 – 1650)

Only put off until tomorrow what you are willing to die having left undone.
Pablo Picasso (1881 – 1973)

Ability is of little account without opportunity.
Napoleon Bonaparte (1769 – 1821)

It's easier to resist at the beginning than at the end.
Leonardo da Vinci (1452 – 1519)

Why does the eye see a thing more clearly in dreams than the imagination when awake?
Leonardo da Vinci (1452 – 1519)

Judge a man by his questions rather than by his answers.
Voltaire (1694 – 1778)

Be yourself; everyone else is already taken.
Oscar Wilde (1854 – 1900)

The man who has no imagination has no wings.
Muhammad Ali (1942 – 2016)

Your intellect may be confused, but your emotions will never lie to you.
Roger Ebert (1942 – 2013)

Everything in moderation, including moderation.
Oscar Wilde (1854 – 1900)

You can pretend to be serious; you can't pretend to be witty.
Sacha Guitry (1885-1957)

I have never in my life learned anything from any man who agreed with me.
Dudley Field Malone (1882 – 1950)

I've learned that people will forget what you said, people will forget what you did, but people will never forget how you made them feel.
Maya Angelou (1928 – 2014)

He who will not reason, is a bigot; he, who cannot, is a fool; and he, who dares not, is a slave.
William Drummond (1585 – 1649)

People will forget what you said. People will forget what you did. But people will never forget how you made them feel.
Maya Angelou (1928 – 2014)

Solitude is a good place to visit but a poor place to stay.
Josh Billings (1818 – 85)

In order to be irreplaceable one must always be different.
Coco Chanel (1883 – 1971)

Never ruin an apology with an excuse.
Benjamin Franklin (1706 -90)

To speak ill of others is a dishonest way of praising ourselves.
Will Durant (1885 – 1981)

What we learn from history is that people don't learn from history.
Warren Buffet (1930 -)

Nothing of me is original. I am the combined effort of everybody I've ever known.
Chuck Palahniuk (1962 -)

The only way to get rid of a temptation is to yield to it.
Oscar Wilde (1854 – 1900)

Lucky fools do not bear the slightest suspicion that they may be lucky fools - by definition, they do not know that they belong to such a category.
Nassim Nicholas Taleb (1960 -)

Common sense and a sense of humor are the same thing, moving at different speeds. A sense of humor is just common sense, dancing.
Clive James (1939 -)

You can be sincere and still be stupid.
Fyodor Dostoyevsky (1821 – 81)

A man's mind is stretched by a new idea or sensation, and never shrinks back to its former dimensions.
Oliver Wendell Holmes Sr. (1809 – 94)

Rudeness is the weak man's imitation of strength.
Edmund Burke (1729 – 97)

I'm afraid of losing my obscurity. Genuineness only thrives in the dark. Like celery.
Aldous Huxley (1894 - 1963)

You can easily judge the character of a man by how he treats those who can do nothing for him.
Johann Wolfgang von Goethe (1749 – 1832)

The mind once enlightened cannot again become dark.
Thomas Paine (1737 – 1809)

Everyone sees what you appear to be, few experience what you really are.
Niccolò Machiavelli (1469 – 1527)

Imagination was given to man to compensate him for what he is not, and a sense of humor was provided to console him for what he is.
Oscar Wilde (1854 – 1900)

In order to keep a true perspective of one's importance, everyone should have a dog that will worship him and a cat that will ignore him.
Dereke Bruce

In the end, we will remember not the words of our enemies, but the silence of our friends.
Martin Luther King Jr. (1929 – 1968)

There is nothing safe about sex. There never will be.
Norman Mailer (1923 – 2007)

Every absurdity has a champion to defend it.
Oliver Goldsmith (1728 – 74)

Always back the horse named self-interest, son. It'll be the only one trying.
Jack Lang (1939 -)

The nearest way to glory is to strive to be what you wish to be thought to be.
Socrates (470 BC – 399 BC)

Experience is not what happens to a man; it is what a man does with what happens to him.
Aldous Huxley (1894 - 1963)

The face is a picture of the mind with the eyes as its interpreter.
Marcus Tullius Cicero (106 BC – 43 BC)

Curiosity has its own reason for existing.
Albert Einstein (1879 - 1955)

Self-respect--the secure feeling that no one, as yet, is suspicious.
H. L. Mencken (1880 - 1956)

INTELLIGENCE

Only two things are infinite, the universe and human stupidity, and I'm not sure about the universe.
Albert Einstein (1879 - 1955)

The conclusion is the place where you got tired of thinking.
Arthur Bloc (1948 -)

Intelligence is the ability to adapt to change.
Stephen Hawking (1942 -)

I can't tell you if genius is hereditary, because heaven has granted me no offspring.
James McNeill Whistler (1834 – 1903)

A great many people think they are thinking when they are actually rearranging their prejudices.
William James (1842-1910)

A concept is a brick. It can be used to build a courthouse of reason. Or it can be thrown through the window.
Gilles Deleuze (1925 – 95)

The clever cat eats cheese and breathes down rat holes with baited breath.
W. C. Fields (1880 – 1946)

Yesterday I was clever, so I wanted to change the world. Today I am wise, so I am changing myself.
Rumi (1207 – 73)

A stupid man's report of what a clever man says can never be accurate, because he unconsciously translates what he hears into something he can understand.
Bertrand Russell (1872 – 1970)

Arguing with a fool proves there are two.
Doris M. Smith

Only the wisest and stupidest of men never change.
Confucius (551 BC – 479 BC)

The highest form of ignorance is when you reject something you don't know anything about.
Wayne Dyer (1940 – 2015)

I not only use all the brains I have, but all that I can borrow.

Woodrow Wilson (1856 – 1924)

Great minds discuss ideas, average minds discuss events, small minds discuss people.
Eleanor Roosevelt (1884 – 1962)

A person hears only what they understand.
Johann Wolfgang von Goethe (1749 – 1832)

Too often we... enjoy the comfort of opinion without the discomfort of thought.
Jack Kennedy (1918 - 63)

We all agree that pessimism is a mark of superior intellect.
John Kenneth Galbraith (1908 – 2006)

Intelligence is an accident of evolution, and not necessarily an advantage.
Isaac Asimov (1920 – 92)

The first ultra-intelligent machine is the last invention that man need ever make, provided that the machine is docile enough to tell us how to keep it under control.
Nick Bostrom (1973 -)

The learned ignore the evidence of their senses to preserve the coherence of the ideas of their imagination.
Adam Smith (1723 – 90)

Reason has always existed, but not always in a reasonable form.
Karl Marx (1818 -83)

Everybody is a genius. But, if you judge a fish by its ability to climb a tree, it will spend its whole life believing that it is stupid.
Albert Einstein (1879 - 1955)

Intelligence is based on how efficient a species became at doing the things they need to survive.
Charles Darwin (1809 -82)

Thoughts are the shadows of our feelings - always darker, emptier and simpler.
Friedrich Nietzsche (1844 – 1900)

There are men who can think no deeper than a fact.
Voltaire (1694 – 1778)

If I had eight hours to chop down a tree, I'd spend six hours sharpening my ax.
Abraham Lincoln (1809 – 65)

The true sign of intelligence is not knowledge but imagination.
Albert Einstein (1879 - 1955)

Prejudices are what fools use for reason.
Voltaire (1694 – 1778)

Great thoughts speak only to the thoughtful mind, but great actions speak to all mankind.
Emily P. Bissell (1861 – 1948)

A thinker sees his own actions as experiments and questions-- as attempts to find out something. Success and failure are for him answers above all.
Friedrich Nietzsche (1844 - 1900)

The trouble with the world is that the stupid are cocksure and the intelligent are full of doubt.
Bertrand Russell (1872 – 1970)

Talent hits a target no one else can hit; Genius hits a target no one else can see.
Arthur Schopenhauer (1788 – 1860)

If everyone is thinking alike, then somebody isn't thinking.
George S. Patton (1885 – 1941)

I suppose it is, if the only tool you have is a hammer, to treat everything as if it were a nail.
Abraham Maslow (1908 -70)

Without deviation from the norm, progress is not possible.
Frank Zappa (1940 – 93)

The third-rate mind is only happy when it is thinking with the majority. The second-rate mind is only happy when it is thinking with the minority. The first-rate mind is only happy when it is thinking.
AA. Milne (1882 – 1956)

You can tell how smart people are by what they laugh at.
Tina Fey (1970 -)

The best minds of my generation are thinking about how to make people click ads. That sucks.
Jeff Hammerbacher (1982 -)

Talent does what it can; genius does what it must.
Edward George Bulwer-Lytton (1803 – 73)

We do not learn from experience... we learn from reflecting on experience.
John Dewey (1859 – 1952)

It requires a very unusual mind to undertake the analysis of the obvious.
Alfred North Whitehead (1861 – 1947)

You might be poor, your shoes might be broken, but your mind is a palace.
Frank McCourt (1930 – 2009)

We should take care not to make the intellect our god; it has, of course, powerful muscles, but no personality.
Albert Einstein (1879 - 1955)

A problem well stated is a problem half solved.
Charles Franklin Kettering (1876-1958)

Simple can be harder than complex; you have to work hard to get your thinking clean to make it simple.
Steve Jobs (1955 – 2011)

Better to remain silent and be thought a fool than to speak out and remove all doubt.
Abraham Lincoln (1809 – 65)

The mark of mediocrity is to look for precedent.
Norman Mailer (1923 – 2007)

The conventional view serves to protect us from the painful job of thinking.
John Kenneth Galbraith (1908 – 2006)

Human beings aren't rational animals; we're rationalizing animals who want to appear reasonable to ourselves.
Eliot Aronson (1932 -)

KNOWLEDGE

How it is we have so much information, but know so little?
Noam Chomsky (1928 -)

If a man will begin with certainties, he shall end in doubts; but if he will be content to begin with doubts he shall end in certainties.
Francis Bacon (1561-1626)

Everything we hear is an opinion, not a fact. Everything we see is a perspective, not the truth.
Marcus Aurelius (121 – 180)

There's a world of difference between truth and facts. Facts can obscure truth.
Maya Angelou (1928 – 2014)

Not ignorance, but ignorance of ignorance is the death of knowledge.
Alfred North Whitehead (1861 – 1947)

Facts do not cease to exist because they are ignored.
Aldous Huxley (1894 - 1963)

If you can't explain it simply, you don't understand it well enough.
Albert Einstein (1879 - 1955)

The fog of information can drive out knowledge.
Daniel J. Boorstin (1914 – 2004)

The only thing I know is that I know nothing.
Socrates (470 BC – 399 BC)

I very rarely think in words at all. A thought comes, and I may try to express it in words afterwards.
Albert Einstein (1879 - 1955)

I am the wisest man alive, for I know one thing, and that is that I know nothing.
Plato (428 BC – 348 BC)

The possible ranks higher than the actual.
Martin Heidegger (1889 – 1976)

The fundamental cause of the trouble is that in the modern world the stupid are cocksure while the intelligent are full of doubt.
Bertrand Russell (1872 – 1970)

It ain't what you know that gets you into trouble. It's what you know for sure that just ain't so.
Mark Twain (1835 – 1910)

Absence of evidence is not evidence of absence.
Carl Sagan (1934 – 96)

For it was my master who taught me not only how very little I knew but also that any wisdom to which I might ever aspire could consist only in realizing more fully the infinity of my ignorance.
Karl Popper (1902 – 94)

Knowledge is the small part of ignorance that we arrange and classify.
Ambrose Bierce (1842 – 1914)

That which can be asserted without evidence, can be dismissed without evidence.
Christopher Hitchens (1949 – 2011)

I learned very early the difference between knowing the name of something and knowing something.
Richard Feynman (1918 – 88)

The larger the island of knowledge, the longer the shoreline of wonder.
Ralph W Stockman (1889 – 1970)

The gift of fantasy has meant more to me than my talent for absorbing positive knowledge.
Albert Einstein (1955 - 1879)

Information is not knowledge.
Albert Einstein (1955 - 1879)

Daring ideas are like chessmen moved forward. They may be beaten, but they may start a winning game.
Johann Wolfgang von Goethe (1749 – 1832)

It is not certain that everything is uncertain.
Blaise Pascal (1623 – 62)

The most incomprehensible thing about the world is that it is at all comprehensible.
Albert Einstein (1879 - 1955)

Whenever a theory appears to you as the only possible one, take this as a sign that you have neither understood the theory nor the problem which it was intended to solve.
Karl Popper (1902 – 94)

Wonder is the beginning of wisdom.
Socrates (470 BC – 399 BC)

All truth passes through three stages. First, it is ridiculed. Second, it is violently opposed. Third, it is accepted as being self-evident.
Arthur Schopenhauer (1788 – 1860)

Prefer knowledge to wealth, for the one is transitory, the other perpetual.
Socrates (470 BC – 399 BC)

Doubt is uncomfortable, certainty is ridiculous.
Voltaire (1694 – 1778)

Wonder is the seed of knowledge.
Francis Bacon (1561 – 1626)

If you leave the smallest corner of your head vacant for a moment, other people's opinions will rush in from all quarters.
George Bernard Shaw (1856 – 1950)

How much easier it is to be critical than to be correct.
Benjamin Disraeli (1804 – 81)

Imagination is more important than knowledge. For knowledge is limited to all we now know and understand, while imagination embraces the entire world, and all there ever will be to know and understand.
Albert Einstein (1879 - 1955)

We don't know a millionth of one percent about anything.
Thomas Alva Edison (1847 – 1931)

An expert is a man who has made all the mistakes which can be made, in a narrow field.
Niels Bohr (1885 – 1962)

There are no facts, only interpretations.
Friedrich Nietzsche (1844 – 1900)

No man's knowledge here can go beyond his experience.
John Locke (1632 – 1704)

While in theory randomness is an intrinsic property, in practice, randomness is incomplete information.
Nassim Nicholas Taleb (1960 -)

What we know is a drop, what we don't know is an ocean.
Isaac Newton (1643 – 1727)

Our knowledge can only be finite, while our ignorance must necessarily be infinite.
Karl Popper (1902 – 94)

When my information changes, I alter my conclusions. What do you do, sir?
John Maynard Keynes (1883 – 1946)

If the human brain were so simple that we could understand it, we would be so simple that we couldn't.
Emerson M. Pugh (1929 -)

The greatest enemy of knowledge is not ignorance; it is the illusion of knowledge.
Stephen Hawking (1942-)

Contradictions do not exist. Whenever you think that you are facing a contradiction, check your premises. You will find that one of them is wrong.
Ayn Rand (1905-1982)

The only source of knowledge is experience.
Albert Einstein (1879 - 1955)

He who knows best knows how little he knows.
Thomas Jefferson (1743 – 1826)

He who knows all the answers has not been asked all the questions.
Confucius (551 BC – 479 BC)

People would rather believe than know.
Edward O. Wilson (1929 -)

We are here and it is now. Further than that, all human knowledge is moonshine.
H. L. Mencken (1880 - 1956)

A point of view can be a dangerous luxury when substituted for insight and understanding.
Marshall McLuhan (1911 - 80)

LAW

Mercy to the guilty is cruelty to the innocent.
Adam Smith (1723 – 90)

It is not wisdom but Authority that makes a law.
Thomas Hobbes (1588 – 1679)

When you go into court you are putting your fate into the hands of twelve people who weren't smart enough to get out of jury duty.
Norm Crosby (1927 -)

A precedent embalms a principle.
Benjamin Disraeli (1804 – 81)

Justice will not be served until those who are unaffected are as outraged as those who are.
Benjamin Franklin (1706 -90)

Injustice anywhere is a threat to justice everywhere.
Martin Luther King Jr. (1929 – 68)

In the absence of justice, what is sovereignty but organized robbery?
St. Augustine (354 – 430)

It depends upon what the meaning of the word 'is' is.
William Jefferson Clinton (1946-)

Feel ashamed to live in a land where justice is a game.
Bob Dylan (1941 -)

Justice delayed is justice denied.
William Ewart Gladstone (1809 – 98)

For the powerful, crimes are those that others commit.
Noam Chomsky (1928 -)

The best way to get a bad law repealed is to enforce it strictly.
Abraham Lincoln (1809 – 65)

Justice is truth in action.
Benjamin Disraeli (1804 – 81)

Nobody gets justice. People only get good luck or bad luck.
Orson Welles (1915 – 85)

A jury consists of twelve persons chosen to decide who has the better lawyer.
Robert Frost (1874 – 1963)

We are in bondage to the law so that we might be free.
Marcus Tullius Cicero (106 BC – 43 BC)

It is forbidden to kill; therefore, all murderers are punished unless they kill in large numbers and to the sound of trumpets.
Voltaire (1694 – 1778)

Laws grind the poor, and rich men rule the law.
Oliver Goldsmith (1728 – 74)

Laws are like cobwebs, which may catch small flies, but let wasps and hornets break through.
Jonathan Swift (1667 – 1745)

A judge is a law student who marks his own examination papers.
H. L. Mencken (1880 - 1956)

Laws are like sausages. It's better not to see them being made.
Otto von Bismarck (1815 - 1898)

Every law is an infraction of liberty.
Jeremy Bentham (1748-1832)

In law, nothing is certain but the expense.
Samuel Butler (1612-1680)

Crime is simply a convenient monosyllable which we apply to what happens when the brain and the heart come into conflict and the brain is defeated.
Arnold Bennett (1867–1931)

Justice is open to everyone in the same way as the Ritz Hotel.
Judge Sturgess

Poverty is the mother of crime.
Marcus Aurelius (121 – 180)

Capital punishment is as fundamentally wrong as a cure for crime as charity is wrong as a cure for poverty.
Henry Ford (1863 – 1947)

An appeal... is when you ask one court to show its contempt for another court.
Finley Peter Dunne (1867 – 1936)

Law applied to its extreme is the greatest injustice.
Marcus Tullius Cicero (106 BC – 43 BC)

LIES

If you tell the truth, you don't have to remember anything.

Mark Twain (1835 – 1910)

The liar's punishment is not in the least that he is not believed, but that he cannot believe anyone else.
George Bernard Shaw (1856 – 1950)

If you tell a lie big enough and keep repeating it, people will eventually come to believe it. The lie can be maintained only for such time as the State can shield the people from the political, economic and/or military consequences of the lie. It thus becomes vitally important for the State to use all of its powers to repress dissent, for the truth is the mortal enemy of the lie, and thus by extension, the truth is the greatest enemy of the State.
Joseph Goebbels (1887 – 1945)

A truth that's told with bad intent
Beats all the lies you can invent.
William Blake (1757 – 1827)

If you have something to say and say nothing, you are really telling a lie.
Ashleigh Brilliant (1933 -)

I'm not upset that you lied to me, I'm upset that from now on I can't believe you.
Friedrich Nietzsche (1844 – 1900)

He who cannot lie does not know what the truth is.
Friedrich Nietzsche (1844 – 1900)

There are a terrible lot of lies going about the world, and the worst of it is that half of them are true.
Winston Churchill (1874 – 1965)

A lie told often enough becomes truth.
Vladimir Lenin (1870 – 1924)

Half of the people lie with their lips; the other half with their tears.
Nassim Nicholas Taleb (1960 -)

We're all islands shouting lies to each other across seas of misunderstanding.
Rudyard Kipling (1865 – 1936)

Above all, don't lie to yourself. The man who lies to himself and listens to his own lie comes to a point that he cannot distinguish the truth within him, or around him, and so loses all respect for himself and for others. And having no respect he ceases to love.
Fyodor Dostoyevsky (1821 – 81)

Repetition does not transform a lie into a truth.
Franklin D Roosevelt (1882 – 1945)

The basic tool for the manipulation of reality is the manipulation of words. If you can control the meaning of words, you can control the people who must use the words.
Philip K. Dick (1928 – 82)

Who controls the past controls the future. Who controls the present controls the past.
George Orwell (1903 -50)

A lie with a purpose is one of the worst kind, and the most profitable.
Finley Peter Dunne (1867 – 1936)

An ambassador is an honest man sent to lie abroad for his country.
Henry Wotton (1568 – 1639)

Tell me anyway - maybe I can find the truth by comparing the lies.
Leon Trotsky (1879 - 1940)

Lying is done with words and also with silence.
Adrienne Rich (1929 – 2012)

People do not believe lies because they have to, but because they want to.
Malcolm Muggeridge (1903 – 90)

The slickest way in the world to lie is to tell the right amount of truth at the right time - and then shut up.
Robert A. Heinlein (1907 – 88)

The cruelest lies are often told in silence.
Robert Louis Stevenson(1850 - 94)

LIFE

Reality is merely an illusion, albeit a very persistent one.
Albert Einstein (1879 - 1955)

Past time is finite, future time is infinite.
Edwin Hubble (1889 - 1953)

Life is not measured by the number of breaths you take but by the moments that take your breath away.
Maya Angelou (1928 – 2014)

I am, somehow, less interested in the weight and convolutions of Einstein's brain than in the near certainty that people of equal talent have lived and died in cotton fields and sweatshops.
Stephen Jay Gould (1941 – 2002)

We are perishing for lack of wonder, not for lack of wonders.
GK Chesterton (1874 – 1936)

Fill the unforgiving minute with sixty seconds worth of distance run.
Rudyard Kipling (1865 – 1931)

In three words I can sum up everything I have learned about life – It goes on.
Robert Frost (1874 – 1963)

Life can only be understood backwards, but it must be lived forward.
Soren Kierkegaard (1813 – 55)

I sit astride life like a bad rider on a horse. I only owe it to the horse's good nature that I am not thrown off at this very moment.
Ludwig Wittgenstein (1889 – 1951)

Fools learn from experience. Wise men learn from the experience of others.
Otto von Bismarck (1815 – 98)

Learning to ignore things is one of the great paths to inner peace.
Robert J. Sawyer (1960 -)

Time is a great healer, but a poor beautician.
Lucille S. Harper (1912 – 95)

Life is a fatal complaint, and an eminently contagious one.
Oliver Wendell Holmes (1809 – 94)

We are all in the gutter, but some of us are looking at the stars.
Oscar Wilde (1854 – 1900)

Life is not so bad if you have plenty of luck, a good physique, and not too much imagination.
Christopher Isherwood (1904 - 86)

It's not that life is so short...It's that you're dead so long.
Mark Whetu

The fact that we live at the bottom of a deep gravity well, on the surface of a gas covered planet going around a nuclear fireball 90 million miles away and think this to be normal is obviously some indication of how skewed our perspective tends to be.
Douglas Adams (1952 – 2011)

Time is a drug. Too much of it kills you.
Terry Pratchett (1948 – 2015)

Our life is frittered away by detail... simplify, simplify.
Henry David Thoreau (1817 - 62)

Life may have no meaning. Or even worse, it may have a meaning of which I disapprove.
Ashleigh Brilliant (1933 -)

What is on a drunken man's lips is on a sober man's mind.
Danish proverb

The long run is a misleading guide to current affairs. In the long run we are all dead.
John Maynard Keynes (1883 – 1946)

Luck is what happens when preparation meets opportunity.
Seneca (4BC – 65 AD)

He who can no longer pause to wonder and stand rapt in awe, is as good as dead; his eyes are closed.
Albert Einstein (1879 - 1955)

Worrying is like paying on a debt that may never come due.
Will Rogers (1879 – 1935)

The unexamined life is not worth living.
Socrates (470 BC – 399 BC)

Life is nasty, brutish, and short.
Thomas Hobbes (1588 – 1679)

Don't ever wrestle with a pig. You'll both get dirty, but the pig will enjoy it.
Cale Yarborough (1939 -)

There are people who, instead of listening to what is being said to them, are already listening to what they are going to say themselves.
Albert Guinon (1863 – 1923)

Sometimes one pays most for the things one gets for nothing.
Albert Einstein (1879 - 1955)

Logic will get you from A to B. Imagination will take you everywhere.
Albert Einstein (1879 - 1955)

I don't know why we are here, but I'm pretty sure that it is not in order to enjoy ourselves.
Ludwig Wittgenstein (1889 – 1951)

It is better to be roughly right than precisely wrong.
John Maynard Keynes (1883 – 1946)

The chicken is only an egg's way for making another egg.
Richard Dawkins (1941 -)

Hope in reality is the worst of all evils, because it prolongs the torments of man.
Friedrich Nietzsche (1844 – 1900)

Virtue is more to be feared than vice, because its excesses are not subject to the regulation of conscience.
Adam Smith (1723 – 90)

Give a man a match, and he'll be warm for a minute, but set him on fire, and he'll be warm for the rest of his life.
Terry Pratchett (1948 – 2015)

Everything that can be counted does not necessarily count; everything that counts cannot necessarily be counted.
Albert Einstein (1879 - 1955)

The optimist thinks this is the best of all possible worlds. The pessimist fears it is true.
J. Robert Oppenheimer (1904 -67)

Life seems but a quick succession of busy nothings.
Jane Austen (1775 – 1817)

Whether you believe you can do a thing or not, you're right.
Henry Ford (1863 – 1947)

Insults are the arguments employed by those who are in the wrong.
Jean-Jacques Rousseau (1712 – 78)

When it is dark enough, you can see the stars.
Ralph Waldo Emerson (1803 – 82)

We are tomorrow's past.
Mary Wollstonecraft Shelley (1797 – 1851)

Nothing in the world is more dangerous than sincere ignorance and conscientious stupidity.
Martin Luther King, Jr. (1929 – 68)

Be the change you want to see in the world.
Mahatma Gandhi (1869 – 1948)

Chance favors the prepared mind.
Louis Pasteur (1822 – 95)

Nothing in life is to be feared. It is only to be understood.
Marie Curie (1867 – 1934)

The man who views the world at 50 the same as he did at 20 has wasted 30 years of his life.
Muhammad Ali (1942 – 2016)

To succeed in life, you need two things; ignorance and confidence.
Mark Twain (1835 – 1910)

Nothing will ever be attempted if all possible objections have to be overcome first.
Samuel Johnson (1709 – 84)

The present moment is the only moment available to us and it is the door to all moments.
Thich Nhat Hank (1926 -)

The purpose of life is a life of purpose.
Robert Byrne (1930 -)

It is never too late to be what you might have been.
George Eliot (1819 – 80)

The future belongs to those who believe in the beauty of their dreams.
Eleanor Roosevelt (1884 – 1962)

If you think in terms of a year, plant a seed; if in terms of ten years, plant trees; if in terms of 100 years, teach the people.
Confucius (551 BC – 479 BC)

Life has meaning only if one barters it day by day for something other than itself.
Antoine de Saint-Exupery (1900 – 44)

Tradition is just the illusion of permanence.
Woody Allen (1935 -)

Not only is the Universe stranger than we think, it is stranger than we can think.
Werner Heisenberg (1901 – 76)

For many events, roughly 80% of the effects come from 20% of the causes.
Vilfredo Pareto (1848 – 1923)

Life is a dream for the wise, a game for the fool, a comedy for the rich, a tragedy for the poor.
Sholom Aleichem (1859 – 1916)

Nobody ever figures out what life is all about, and it doesn't matter. Explore the world. Nearly everything is really interesting if you go into it deeply enough.
Richard Feynman (1918 – 88)

Lost time is never found again.
Benjamin Franklin (1706 – 90)

It is good to have an end to journey toward; but it is the journey that matters, in the end
Ernest Hemmingway (1899 – 1961)

Things may come to those who wait...but only the things left by those who hustle.
Abraham Lincoln (1809 – 65)

Suspect each moment, for it is a thief, tiptoeing away with more than it brings.
John Updike (1932 – 2009)

Form may be of more account than substance. A lens of ice will focus a solar beam to a blaze.
George Iles (1960 -)

I believe that imagination is stronger than knowledge - myth is more potent than history - dreams are more powerful than facts - hope always triumphs over experience - laughter is the cure for grief - love is stronger than death.
Robert Fulghum (1937 -)

Expect the best. Prepare for the worst. Capitalize on what comes.
Zig Ziglar (1928 - 2012)

The chief beauty about time is that you cannot waste it in advance.
Arnold Bennett (1867–1931)

No one ever told me that grief felt so like fear.
C.S. Lewis (1898 – 1963)

To enjoy the flavor of life, take big bites. Moderation is for monks.
Robert A. Heinlein (1907 – 88)

Change is the law of life. And those who look only to the past or present are certain to miss the future.
John Fitzgerald Kennedy (1917 – 63)

Things do not change; we change.
Henry David Thoreau (1817 - 62)

LITERATURE

A book is like a garden carried in the pocket.
Arabian Proverb

For books are more than books, they are the life, the very heart and core of ages past, the reason why men worked and died, the essence and quintessence of their lives.
Marcus Tullius Cicero (106 BC – 43 BC)

The man who does not read books has no advantage over the man that cannot read them.
Mark Twain (1835 – 1910)

Poetry is when an emotion has found its thought and the thought has found words.
Robert Frost (1874 – 1963)

Books are immortal sons deifying their sires.
Plato (428 BC – 348 BC)

What literature can and should do is change the people who teach the people who don't read the books.
AS Byatt (1936 -)

There are two motives for reading a book; one, that you enjoy it; the other, that you can boast about it.
Bertrand Russell (1872 – 1970)

There is nothing to writing. All you do is sit down at a typewriter and bleed.
Ernest Hemingway (1899 – 1961)

We write to taste life twice, in the moment and in retrospect.
Anaïs Nin (1903 – 77)

The ink of the scholar is more holy than the blood of the martyr.
Muhammad (570 – 632)

Thank you for sending me a copy of your book - I'll waste no time reading it.
Moses Hadas (1900 – 66)

Words are, of course, the most powerful drug used by mankind.
Rudyard Kipling (1865 – 1936)

Reading without reflecting is like eating without digesting.
Edmund Burke (1729 – 97)

What is written without effort is in general read without pleasure.
Samuel Johnson (1709 – 84)

Some books should be tasted, some devoured, but only a few should be chewed and digested thoroughly.
Francis Bacon (1561 – 1626)

The reading of all good books is like conversation with the finest men of past centuries.
Rene Descartes (1596 – 1650)

Beware the man of a single book.
Thomas Aquinas (1225 – 74)

I heard someone tried the monkeys-on-typewriters bit trying for the plays of W. Shakespeare, but all they got was the collected works of Francis Bacon.
Bill Hirst

Criticism is prejudice made plausible.
H. L. Mencken (1880 -1956)

Every man's memory is his private literature.
Aldous Huxley (1894 - 1963)

Originality is the art of concealing your sources.
Benjamin Franklin (1706 -90)

No tears in the writer, no tears in the reader. No surprise in the writer, no surprise in the reader.
Robert Frost (1874 – 1963)

Writing is easy. All you have to do is cross out the wrong words.
Mark Twain (1835 – 1910)

Critics are men who watch a battle from a high place then come down and shoot the survivors.
Ernest Hemmingway (1899 – 1963)

Writing books is the closest men ever come to childbearing.
Norman Mailer (1923 – 2007)

Books can be dangerous. The best ones should be labeled. This could change your life.
Helen Exley (1943 -)

One glance at a book and you hear the voice of another person, perhaps someone dead for 1,000 years. To read is to voyage through time.
Carl Sagan (1934 – 96)

Think before you speak. Read before you think.
Fran Lebowitz (1950)

Words can be like X-rays if you use them properly - they'll go through anything. You read and you're pierced.

Aldous Huxley (1894 - 1963)

Man reading should be man intensely alive. The book should be a ball of light in one's hand.

Ezra Pound (1885 – 1972)

A room without books is like a body without a soul.

Marcus Tullius Cicero (106 BC – 43 BC)

Books, the children of the brain.

Jonathan Swift (1667 – 1745)

Reading maketh a full man; conference a ready man; and writing an exact man.

Francis Bacon (1561-1626)

LOVE

The one who loves least controls the relationship.
Anon

Never allow someone to be your priority while allowing yourself to be their option.
Mark Twain (1835 – 1910)

The love that lasts the longest is the love that is never returned.
William Somerset Maugham (1874 – 1965)

Of all forms of caution, caution in love is perhaps the most fatal to true happiness.
Bertrand Russell (1872 – 1970)

Blessed are the hearts that can bend; they shall never be broken.
Albert Camus (1913 – 60)

There is always some madness in love. But there is also always some reason in madness.
Friedrich Nietzsche (1844 – 1900)

Love is a state in which a man sees things most decidedly as they are not.
Friedrich Nietzsche (1844 – 1900)

We look forward to the time when the Power of Love will replace the Love of Power. Then will our world know the blessings of peace.
William Ewart Gladstone (1809 – 98)

Absence diminishes mediocre passions and increases great ones, as the wind blows out candles and fans fire.
François de La Rochefoucauld François (1613 – 80)

Love without sacrifice is like theft.
Nassim Nicholas Taleb (1960 -)

We are never so defenseless against suffering as when we love.
Sigmund Freud (1856 – 1939)

The heart has its reasons which reason knows not.
Blaise Pascal (1623 – 62)

Darkness cannot drive out darkness: only light can do that. Hate cannot drive out hate: only love can do that.
Martin Luther King Jr. (1929 – 68)

Love is an irresistible desire to be irresistibly desired.
Robert Frost (1874 – 1963)

When you fish for love, bait with your heart, not your brain.
Mark Twain (1835 – 1910)

I see when men love women they give but a little of their lives, but women, when they love, give everything.
Oscar Wilde (1854 – 1900)

Women are happier in the love they inspire than in that which they feel; men are just the contrary.
E. P. Beauchene (1874 – 1923)

Falling in love consists merely in uncorking the imagination and bottling the common sense.
Helen Rowland (1875 – 1950)

The opposite of love is not hate, its indifference.
Elie Wiesel (1928 -)

Sex is like money; only too much is enough.
John Updike (1932 – 2009)

In love, women are professionals, men are amateurs.
Francois Truffaut (1932 – 84)

Love is the condition in which the happiness of another person is essential to your own.
Robert A. Heinlein (1907 – 88)

Love is like an hourglass, with the heart filling up as the brain empties.
Jules Renard (1864 – 1910)

MARRIAGE

No man is truly married until he understands every word his wife is not saying.
Anon

A man likes his wife to be just clever enough to appreciate his cleverness, and just stupid enough to admire it.
Israel Zangwill (1864 -1926)

By all means marry; if you get a good wife, you'll become happy; if you get a bad one, you'll become a philosopher.
Socrates (470 BC – 399 BC)

He that displays too often his wife and his wallet is in danger of having both of them borrowed.
Benjamin Franklin (1706 -90)

Marriage is like putting your hand into a bag of snakes in the hope of pulling out an eel.
Leonardo da Vinci (1452 – 1519)

Women marry men hoping they will change. Men marry women hoping they will not. So each is inevitably disappointed.
Albert Einstein (1879-1955)

Assumptions are the termites of relationships.
Henry Winkler (1945-)

Marriage is very difficult. It's like a 5,000–piece jigsaw puzzle, all sky.
Cathy Ladman (1955-)

Nobody will ever win the battle of the sexes. There's too much fraternizing with the enemy.
Henry Kissinger (1923-)

Silence is argument carried out by other means.
Ernesto"Che"Guevara (1928 - 67)

Never make someone a priority when all you are to them is an option.
Maya Angelou (1928 – 2014)

The happiest time of anyone's life is just after the first divorce.
JK Galbraith (1898 – 2006)

Marriage is the only war in which you sleep with the enemy.
French proverb

Pleasure for one hour, a bottle of wine. Pleasure for one year a marriage; but pleasure for a lifetime, a garden.
Erica Jong (1942 -)

Marriage is popular because it combines the maximum of temptation with the maximum of opportunity.
George Bernard Shaw (1856 – 1950)

Chains do not hold a marriage together. It is threads, hundreds of tiny threads which sew people together through the years. That is what makes a marriage last, more than passion or even sex.
Simone Signoret (1921 - 85)

Marriage - a book of which the first chapter is written in poetry and the remaining chapters in prose.
Beverley Nichols (1898 – 1983)

Marriage is the only adventure open to the cowardly.
Voltaire (1694 – 1778)

It is a truth universally acknowledged that a single man in possession of a good fortune must be in want of a wife.
Jane Austen (1775 – 1817)

The trouble is not that I am single and likely to stay single, but that I am lonely and likely to stay lonely.
Charlotte Brontë (1816 – 55)

Marriage is a lottery, but you can't tear up your ticket if you lose.
Jerry Lewis (1926 -)

An intellectual is a person who has discovered something more interesting than sex.
Aldous Huxley (1894 - 1963)

MEDIA

The medium is the message.
Marshall McLuhan (1911 -80)

In America journalism is apt to be regarded as an extension of history: in Britain, as an extension of conversation.
Anthony Sampson (1926-2004)

News is history shot on the wing.
Gene Fowler (1890-1960)

America is a country of inventors, and the greatest of inventors are the newspaper men.
Alexander Graham Bell (1847-1922)

Watching television is like taking black spray paint to your third eye.
Bill Hicks (1961-94)

Once a newspaper touches a story, the facts are lost forever, even to the protagonists.
Norman Mailer (1923-2007)

The man who reads nothing at all is better educated than the man who reads nothing but newspapers.
Thomas Jefferson (1743 – 1826)

All media exist to invest our lives with artificial perceptions and arbitrary values.
Marshall McLuhan (1911 - 80)

MEN

If you want to know what a man's like, take a good look at how he treats his inferiors, not his equals.
JK Rowling (1965-)

A man's heart may have a secret sanctuary where only one woman may enter, but it is full of little anterooms which are seldom vacant.
Helen Rowland (1875-1950)

That is the great distinction between the sexes. Men see objects, women see the relationships between objects.
John Fowles (1926-2005)

Men are governed by lines of intellect - women: by curves of emotion.
James Joyce (1882-1941)

Men are moved by two levers only: fear and self-interest.
Napoleon Bonaparte (1769-1821)

Who loves not wine, women and song, remains a fool his whole life long.
Martin Luther (1929-68)

Men fall in love with their eyes. Women fall in love with their ears.
Phil McGraw (1950-)

Men have become the tools of their tools.
Henry David Thoreau (1817-62)

A man attaches himself to woman -- not to enjoy her, but to enjoy himself.
Simone de Beauvoir (1908-86)

Men are driven by two principal impulses, either by love or by fear.
Niccolò Machiavelli (1429-1527)

The men who cannot laugh at themselves frighten me even more than those who laugh at everything.
Anne Perry (1938 -)

Men play the game; women know the score.
Roger Woddis (1917 – 93)

The follies which a man regrets most, in his life, are those he didn't commit when he had the opportunity.
Helen Rowland (1875 – 1950)

Among men, sex sometimes results in intimacy; among women, intimacy sometimes results in sex.
Barbara Cartland (1901 – 2000)

The only time a woman really succeeds in changing a man is when he is a baby.
Natalie Wood (1938 – 81)

MIDDLE AGE

At eighteen our visions are hills from which we look; at forty-five they are caves in which we hide.
F Scott Fitzgerald (1896-1940)

We shape our tools and thereafter our tools shape us.
Marshall McLuhan (1911 -80)

When I was young, I admired clever people. Now that I am old, I admire kind people.
Abraham Joshua Heschel (1907-1972)

The years teach much which the days never knew.
Ralph Waldo Emerson (1803-82)

Some people die at 25 and aren't buried until 75.
Benjamin Franklin (1706 -90)

You are only young once, but you can stay immature indefinitely.
Ogden Nash (1902-71)

The old believe everything, the middle-aged suspect everything, the young know everything.
Oscar Wilde (1854-1900)

A man who views the world the same at 50 as he did at 20 has wasted 30 years of his life.
Muhammad Ali (1942-2016)

Count your age by friends, not years. Count your life by smiles, not tears.
John Lennon (1940-80)

As I get older I notice the years less and the seasons more.
John Hubbard (1973-)

The older I grow, the more I distrust the familiar doctrine that age brings wisdom.
Henry Louis Mencken (1880 – 1956)

Old age is the only disease you don't want to be cured of.
Orson Welles (1915 – 85)

Every man desires to live long, but no man wishes to be old.
Jonathan Swift (1667 – 1745)

MONEY

To be clever enough to get all that money, one must be stupid enough to want it.
Gilbert K. Chesterton (1874-1936)

You never see a bookie on a bike
Anon

A poor man with weird habits is an idiot, a rich man with weird habits is eccentric.
Anon

Markets can remain irrational longer than you can remain solvent.
John Maynard Keynes (1883 – 1946)

Debt is the worst poverty.
Thomas Fuller (1608-61)

Nothing sedates rationality like large doses of effortless money.
Warren Buffet (1930 -)

The conspicuously wealthy turn up urging the character building values of the privation of the poor.
John Kenneth Galbraith (1908 – 2006)

If you owe your bank a hundred pounds, you have a problem. But if you owe a million, it has.
John Maynard Keynes (1883 – 1946)

Very few people can afford to be poor.
George Bernard Shaw (1856-1950)

Content makes poor men rich; discontent makes rich men poor.
Benjamin Franklin (1706 -90)

The surest way to remain poor is to be honest.
Napoleon Bonaparte (1769-1821)

He who wishes to be rich in a day will be hanged in a year.
Leonardo da Vinci (1452-1519)

The only foolproof path to wealth is inheritance.
David Gardner (1966-)

I will tell you how to become rich. Close the doors. Be fearful when others are greedy. Be greedy when others are fearful.
Warren Buffet (1930 -)

It is better to have a permanent income than to be fascinating.
Oscar Wilde (1854-1900)

If you understand compound interest, you basically understand the universe.
Robert Brault (1963-)

The greatest wealth is to live content with little.
Plato (428 BC – 348 BC)

There's no such thing as a free lunch.
Milton Friedman (1912-2006)

I like to pay taxes. With them, I buy civilization.
Oliver Wendell Holmes Jr. (1841-1935)

We are not rich by what we possess but by what we can do without.
Immanuel Kant (1724-1802)

Time is more valuable than money. You can get more money, but you cannot get more time.
Jim Rohn (1930 – 2009)

I think the person who takes a job in order to live - that is to say, for the money - has turned himself into a slave.
Joseph Campbell (1904 -87)

Three groups spend other people's money: children, thieves, politicians. All three need supervision.
Dick Armey (1940 -)

A rich man is nothing but a poor man with money.
WC Fields (1880 – 1946)

The best way to help the poor is not to become one of them.
Lang Hancock (1909 – 92)

In the short term, the market is a popularity contest. In the long term, the market is a weighing machine.
Warren Buffet (1930 -)

Inflation is taxation without legislation.
Milton Friedman (1912 – 2006)

The greater the wealth the thicker will be the dirt.
JK Galbraith (1908 – 2006)

MORALITY

The Seven Social Sins are:

Wealth without work.
Pleasure without conscience.
Knowledge without character.
Commerce without morality.
Science without humanity.
Worship without sacrifice.
Politics without principle.
Frederick Lewis Donaldson (1860 -1 1953)

I would never die for my beliefs because I might be wrong.
Bertrand Russell (1872-1970)

Expecting the world to treat you fairly because you are good is
like expecting the bull not to charge because you are a
vegetarian.
Dennis Wholey (1939-)

Every man is guilty of all the good he didn't do.
Voltaire (1694 – 1778)

No snowflake in an avalanche ever feels responsible.
Voltaire (1694 – 1778)

Great and good are seldom the same man.
Winston Churchill (1874-1965)

I do not see why man should not be just as cruel as nature.
Adolf Hitler (1889-1945)

A perfection of means, and confusion of aims, seems to be our main problem.
Albert Einstein (1879 - 1955)

When morality comes up against profit, it is seldom that profit loses.
Shirley Chisholm (1924 – 2005)

Two things awe me most, the starry sky above me and the moral law within me.
Immanuel Kant (1724-1804)

It is the cause and not the death that makes the martyr.
Napoleon Bonaparte (1769 -1821)

The dread of evil is a much more forcible principle of human actions than the prospect of good.
John Locke (1632-1704)

Our scientific power has outrun our spiritual power. We have guided missiles and misguided men.
Martin Luther King, Jr. (1929-68)

Moral indignation is jealousy with a halo.
H. G. Wells (1866-1946)

The atheist is cheating whenever he makes a moral judgment, acting as though it has an objective reference, when his philosophy in fact precludes it.
William A. Dembski (1960-)

The modern conservative is engaged in one of man's oldest exercises in moral philosophy; that is, the search for a superior moral justification for selfishness.
John Kenneth Galbraith (1908-2006)

From the saintly and single-minded idealist to the fanatic is often but a step.
Friedrich Hayek (1899-1992)

A man is usually more careful of his money than he is of his principles.
Ralph Waldo Emerson (1803 – 82)

Virtue has never been as respectable as money.
Mark Twain (1835 – 1910)

We make the future sustainable when we invest in the poor, not when we insist on their suffering.
Bill Gates (1955 -)

Service is the rent that you pay for room on this earth.
Shirley Chisholm (1924 – 2005)

The white man's happiness cannot be purchased by the black man's misery.
Frederick Douglas (1818 – 95)

We fought a war on poverty, and poverty won.
Ronald Reagan (1911 – 2004)

To educate a man in mind and not in morals is to educate a menace to society.
Teddy Roosevelt (1858 – 1919)

When you give food to the poor, they call you a saint. When you ask why the poor have no food, they call you a communist.
Archbishop Helder Camara (1909 -99)

Political correctness does not legislate tolerance; it only organizes hatred.
Jacques Barzun (1907 – 2012)

People never lie so much as after a hunt, during a war or before an election.
Otto von Bismarck (1815 -98)

A statesman is a successful politician who is dead.
Thomas Brackett Reed (1839 – 1902)

Men, their rights, and nothing more; women, their rights, and nothing less.
Susan B Anthony (1820 – 1906)

In matters of style, swim with the current; in matters of principle, stand like a rock.
Thomas Jefferson (1743 – 1826)

The said truth is that it is the greatest happiness of the greatest number that is the measure of right and wrong
.Jeremy Bentham (1748-1832)

The end may justify the means as long as there is something that justifies the end.
Leon Trotsky (1879 - 1940)

Do not be too moral. You may cheat yourself out of much life so. Aim above morality. Be not simply good, be good for something.
Henry David Thoreau (1817 - 62)

MUSIC

If I were not a physicist, I would probably be a musician. I often think in music. I live my daydreams in music. I see my life in terms of music. ... I get most joy in life out of music.
Albert Einstein (1879 - 1955)

Music expresses that which cannot be said and on which it is impossible to be silent.
Victor Hugo (1802-85)

Life seems to go on without effort when I am filled with music.
George Eliot (1819-80)

Music is spiritual. The music business is not.
Van Morrison (1945 -)

Anything that is too stupid to be spoken is sung.
Voltaire (1694 – 1778)

After silence, that which comes nearest to expressing the inexpressible is music.
Aldous Huxley (1894 - 1963)

Music is what feelings sound like.
Georgia Cates (1975 -)

Those who danced were thought to be quite insane by those who could not hear the music.
Angela Monet

Words make you think a thought. Music makes you feel a feeling. A song makes you feel a thought.
E. Y. Harburg (1896 – 1981)

Music is the art of thinking with sounds.
Jules Combarieu (1859 – 1916)

Music is the universal language of mankind.
Henry Wadsworth Longfellow (1807 – 82)

Music, the mosaic of the air
Andrew Marvell (1621 – 78)

Music is the wine that fills the cup of silence.
Robert Fripp (1946 -)

A painter paints pictures on canvas. But musicians paint their pictures on silence.
Leopold Stokowski (1882 – 1977)

PEACE

One man builds a bridge; a thousand men cross it.
Uzbek proverb

It is more difficult to organize a peace than to win a war; but the fruits of victory will be lost if the peace is not organized.
Aristotle (384 BC – 322 BC)

They make a desert and call it peace.
Tacitus (56-120)

The absence of war is not peace.
Harry S Truman (1884-1972)

We prefer world law in the age of self-determination to world war in the age of mass extermination.
Jack Kennedy (1918 - 63)

An appeaser is one who feeds a crocodile, hoping it will eat him last.
Winston S. Churchill (1874 – 1965)

There is no way to peace, peace is the way.
A. J. Muste (1885 – 1967)

If war is ever lawful, then peace is sometimes sinful.
C.S. Lewis (1898 – 1963)

You can have peace. Or you can have freedom. Don't ever count on having both at once.
Robert A. Heinlein (1907 – 88)

Peace is a daily, a weekly, a monthly process, gradually changing opinions, slowly eroding old barriers, quietly building new structures.

John Fitzgerald Kennedy (1917 – 63)

PHILOSOPHY

Simplicity is about subtracting the obvious and adding the meaningful.
John Maeda (1966-)

In theory there is no difference between theory and practice. But in practice there is.
Jan van de Snepscheut (1953-94)

A philosopher is a blind man in a dark room looking for a black cat that isn't there. A theologian is the man who finds it.
H. L. Mencken (1880 - 1956)

The limits of my language are the limits of my mind. All I know is what I have words for.
Ludwig Wittgenstein (1889 – 1951)

I am an old man and have known a great many troubles, but most of them never happened.
Mark Twain (1835-1910)

Life is only a dream and we are the imagination of ourselves.
Bill Hicks (1961-94)

I'm tired of this back-slappin' "isn't humanity neat" bullshit. We're a virus with shoes.
Bill Hicks (1961-94)

When we are headed the wrong way, the last thing we need is progress.
Nick Bostrom (1973-)

Hundreds of people can talk for one who can think, but thousands can think for one who can see. To see clearly is poetry, prophecy, religion, all in one.
John Ruskin. (1819-1900)

I have nothing, owe a great deal, and the rest I leave to the poor.
Rabelais (1494-1553)

Probably one of the most private things in the world is an egg before it is broken.
M.F.K. Fisher (1908-92)

The early bird may get the worm, but the second mouse gets the cheese.
Stephen Wright (1955-)

Logic takes care of itself; all we have to do is to look and see how it does it.
Ludwig Wittgenstein (1889 – 1951)

Whenever you find yourself on the side of the majority, it is time to pause and reflect.
Mark Twain (1835-1910)

We don't see things as they are. We see them as we are.
Anais Nin (1903-1977)

You see things; and you say 'Why?' But I dream things that never were; and I say 'Why not?'
George Bernard Shaw (1856-1950)

Philosophy is questions that may never be answered. Religion is answers that may never be questioned.
Anon

The first step towards philosophy is incredulity.
Denis Diderot (1713-84)

A cleric who loses his faith abandons his calling; a philosopher who loses his redefines his subject.
Ernest Gellner

The point of philosophy is to start with something so simple as to seem not worth stating, and to end with something so paradoxical that no one will believe it.
Bertrand Russell (1872-1970)

The art of simplicity is a puzzle of complexity.
Doug Horton (1891-1968)

What happens to the hole when the cheese is gone?
Bertolt Brecht (1898-1956)

Do not seek to follow in the footsteps of the men of old; seek what they sought.
Basho (1644-94)

Philosophy is like trying to open a safe with a combination lock: each little adjustment of the dials seems to achieve nothing, only when everything is in place does the door open.
Ludwig Wittgenstein (1889 – 1951)

Philosophy begins in wonder.
Plato (428 BC – 348 BC)

To choose doubt as a philosophy of life is akin to choosing immobility as a means of transportation.
Yann Martel (1963-)

A man with one watch knows what time it is; a man with two watches is never quite sure.
Lee Segall (1945-)

Whereof one cannot speak, thereof one must be silent.
Ludwig Wittgenstein (1889 – 1951)

One cannot step twice in the same river.
Heraclitus (535 BC – 475 BC)

Science is what you know. Philosophy is what you don't know.
Bertrand Russell (1872-1970)

Everything that exists is born for no reason, carries on living through weakness, and dies by accident.
Jean-Paul Sartre (1905-80)

Generally speaking, the errors in religion are dangerous; those in philosophy only ridiculous.
David Hume (1711-76)

..the only simplicity to be trusted is the simplicity to be found on the far side of complexity.
Alfred North Whitehead (1861-1947)

Making itself intelligible is suicide for philosophy.
Martin Heidegger (1889-1976)

The course of every intellectual, if he pursues his journey long and unflinchingly enough, ends in the obvious, from which the non-intellectuals have never stirred.
Aldous Huxley (1894-1963)

Philosophy of science is about as useful to scientists as ornithology is to birds.
Richard Feynman (1918 – 88)

My advice to you is not to inquire why or whither, but just enjoy your ice cream while it's on your plate - that's my philosophy.
Thornton Wilder (1897 – 1975)

To study philosophy is nothing but to prepare one's self to die.
Marcus Tullius Cicero (106 BC – 43 BC)

POLITICS

When I give food to the poor, they call me a saint. When I ask why the poor have no food, they call me a communist.
Hélder Câmara (1909-99)

Democracy is the art and science of running the circus from the monkey-cage.
H. L. Mencken (1880 - 1956)

Man will never be free until the last king is strangled with the entrails of the last priest.
Denis Diderot (1713-84)

No one is free, even the birds are chained to the sky
Bob Dylan (1941 -)

If you think you're free, there's no escape possible.
Ram Dass (1931-)

What you discover in a democracy is that it is difficult to build a house when each nail has an opinion.
Robert Brault (1963-)

He who has a why can endure any how.
Friedrich Nietzsche (1844 – 1900)

The reason they call it the American Dream is because you have to be asleep to believe it.
George Carlin (1937-2008)

Politics is war without bloodshed while war is politics with bloodshed.
Mao Tse-Tung (1893-1976)

I like small British ideas. Big ideas murdered my grandmother.
Daniel Finkelstein (1962-)

Those who can make you believe absurdities can make you commit atrocities.
Voltaire (1694 – 1778)

A diplomat is someone who can tell you to go to hell in such a way that you will look forward to the trip.
Caskie Stinnett (1911 – 98)

The political problem of mankind is to combine three things: economic efficiency, social justice and individual liberty.
John Maynard Keynes (1883-1946)

The rights of every man are diminished when the rights of one man are threatened.
John F. Kennedy (1917 – 63)

Whatever is my right as a man is also the right of another; and it becomes my duty to guarantee as well as to possess.
Thomas Paine (1737-1809)

In politics we presume that everyone who knows how to get votes knows how to administer a city or a state. When we are ill... we do not ask for the handsomest physician, or the most eloquent one.
Plato (428 BC – 348 BC)

You can fool some of the people all of the time, and all of the people some of the time, but you cannot fool all of the people all of the time.
Abraham Lincoln (1809-65)

When the debate is lost, slander becomes the tool of the loser.
Socrates (470 BC - 399 BC)

Politics is the art of choosing between the disastrous and the unpalatable.
John Kenneth Galbraith (1908-2006)

If anything is certain, it is that I myself am not a Marxist.
Karl Marx (1818-83)

Illegal aliens have always been a problem in the United States. Ask any Indian.
Robert Orben (1927 -)

Few are open to conviction, but the majority of men are open to persuasion.
Johann Wolfgang von Goethe (1749 – 1832)

There are some that only employ words for the purpose of disguising their thoughts.
Voltaire (1694 – 1778)

Never hold discussions with the monkey when the organ grinder is in the room.
Winston Churchill (1874-1965)

In politics stupidity is not a handicap.
Napoleon Bonaparte (1769-1821)

Jesus was the first socialist, the first to seek a better life for mankind.
Mikhail Gorbachev (1931-)

Nationalism is an infantile sickness. It is the measles of the human race.
Albert Einstein (1880-1952)

Politicians and diapers have one thing in common. They should both be changed regularly, and for the same reason.
José Maria de Eça de Queiroz (1845-1900)

If you want to make enemies, try to change something.
Woodrow Wilson (1856-1924)

Do you know what we call opinion in the absence of evidence? We call it prejudice.
Michael Crichton (1942-2008)

If an injury has to be done to a man it should be so severe that his vengeance need not be feared.
Niccolo Machiavelli (1469 – 1527)

What is objectionable, what is dangerous about extremists is not that they are extreme, but that they are intolerant.
Robert F. Kennedy (1925-68)

I have a dream that one day little black boys and girls will be holding hands with little white boys and girls.
Martin Luther King Jr. (1929-68)

Freedom is what you do with what's been done to you.
Jean-Paul Sartre (1905-80)

If you want things to stay the same things will have to change.
Giuseppe Tomasi di Lampedusa (1896-1957)

Political correctness is tyranny with manners.
Charlton Heston (1923-2008)

Political power grows out of the barrel of a gun.
Mao Tse-tung (1893 – 1976)

He can compress the most words into the smallest idea of any man I know.
Abraham Lincoln (1809-65)

People demand freedom of speech as a compensation for the freedom of thought which they seldom use.
Søren Kierkegaard (1813-55)

Man is born free, and everywhere he is in chains.
Jean-Jacques Rousseau (1712-88)

The Constitution only guarantees the American people the right to pursue happiness. You have to catch it yourself.
Benjamin Franklin (1706-90)

Politics is the art of looking for trouble, finding it, misdiagnosing it, and then misapplying the wrong remedies.
Groucho Marx (1890 – 1977)

Government exists to protect us from each other. Where government has gone beyond its limits is in deciding to protect us from ourselves.
Ronald Reagan (1911 – 2004)

The best political weapon is the weapon of terror. Cruelty commands respect. Men may hate us. But, we don't ask for their love; only for their fear.
Heinrich Himmler (1900 – 45)

Politics is the gentle art of getting votes from the poor and campaign funds from the rich, by promising to protect each from the other.
Oscar Ameringer (1870 – 1943)

The smart way to keep people passive and obedient is to strictly limit the spectrum of acceptable opinion, but allow very lively debate within that spectrum.
Noam Chomsky (1928 -)

I would rather have questions that can't be answered than answers that can't be questioned.
Richard Feynman (1918 – 88)

A genuine leader is not a searcher for consensus but a molder of consensus.
Martin Luther King Jr. (1929 – 68)

Politics is the art of postponing decisions until they are no longer relevant.
Henri Queuille (1884 – 1970)

It is hard to imagine a more stupid or more dangerous way of making decisions than by putting those decisions in the hands of people who pay no price for being wrong.
Thomas Sowell (1930 -)

In order to become the master, the politician poses as the servant.
Charles de Gaulle (1890 – 1970)

Politicians are not born; they are excreted.
Marcus Tullius Cicero (106 BC – 43 BC)

The best argument against democracy is a five-minute conversation with the average voter.

Winston Churchill (1874 - 1965)

Democracy is a pathetic belief in the collective wisdom of individual ignorance. No one in this world, so far as I know— and I have researched the records for years, and employed agents to help me—has ever lost money by underestimating the intelligence of the great masses of the plain people. Nor has anyone ever lost public office thereby.

H. L. Mencken (1880 - 1956)

RELIGION

Is man merely a mistake of God's? Or God merely a mistake of man's?
Friedrich Nietzsche (1844 – 1900)

We regard God as an airman regards his parachute; it's there for emergencies, but he hopes he'll never have to use it.
C.S. Lewis (1898 – 1963)

I go to seek a Great Perhaps.
François Rabelais (1493-1553)

It is the glory of God to conceal a thing: but the honor of kings is to search out a matter.
Hebrew Proverb

I once prayed to god for a bike, but quickly found out he didn't work that way...so I stole a bike and prayed for his forgiveness.
Emo Philips (1956-)

Belief gets in the way of learning.
Robert Heinlein (1907-88)

Faith may be defined briefly as an illogical belief in the occurrence of the improbable.
H. L. Mencken (1880 - 1956)

Religion stills a thinking mind.
Greg Erwin

Religion is regarded by the common people as true, by the wise as false, and by the rulers as useful.
Seneca (4 BC – 65)

It is an interesting and demonstrable fact, that all children are atheists and were religion not inculcated into their minds, they would remain so.
Ernestine Rose (1810-92)

Religion is what keeps the poor man from murdering the rich.
Napoleon Bonaparte (1769-1821)

God has no religion.
Mahatma Gandhi (1869-1948)

Every religion in the world that has destroyed people is based on love.
Anton LaVey (1930-97)

Religion is a culture of faith; science is a culture of doubt.
Richard Feynman (1918-88)

We are all atheists about most of the gods that humanity has ever believed in. Some of us just go one god further.
Richard Dawkins (1941-)

We must respect the other fellow's religion, but only in the sense and to the extent that we respect his theory that his wife is beautiful and his children smart.
H. L. Mencken (1880 – 1956)

Religion is about turning untested belief into unshakable truth through the power of institutions and the passage of time.
Richard Dawkins (1941-)

I still say a church steeple with a lightning rod on top shows a lack of confidence.
Doug McLeod (1946-)

Men will never be free until the last king is strangled with the entrails of the last priest.
Denis Diderot (1713-84)

The opposite of the religious fanatic is not the fanatical atheist but the gentle cynic who cares not whether there is a god or not.
Eric Hoffer (1898-1983)

The less you know, the more you believe.
Bono (1960-)

What really interests me is whether God had any choice in the creation of the world.
Albert Einstein (1879 - 1955)

If there were no God, it would have been necessary to invent him.
Voltaire (1694 – 1778)

It is always more difficult to fight against faith than against knowledge.
Adolf Hitler (1889-1945)

For a truly religious man nothing is tragic.
Ludwig Wittgenstein (1889 – 1951)

Religion is the impotence of the human mind to deal with occurrences it cannot understand.
Karl Marx (1818-83)

I am against religion because it teaches us to be satisfied with not understanding the world.
Richard Dawkins (1941-)

The truths of religion are never so well understood as by those who have lost their power of reasoning.
Voltaire (1694 – 1778)

The fact that a believer is happier than a skeptic is no more to the point than the fact than a drunken man is happier than a sober one.
George Bernard Shaw (1856-1950)

I am a deeply religious nonbeliever - This is a somewhat new kind of religion.
Albert Einstein (1879 - 1955)

This most beautiful system [The Universe] could only proceed from the dominion of an intelligent and powerful Being.
Isaac Newton (1643-1727)

To one who has faith, no explanation is necessary. To one without faith, no explanation is possible.
St. Thomas Aquinas (1225 - 74)

Just as no one can be forced into belief, so no one can be forced into unbelief.
Sigmund Freud (1856-1939)

I had to deny knowledge in order to make room for faith.
Immanuel Kant (1724-1804)

I like your Christ, I do not like your Christians. Your Christians are so unlike your Christ.
Mahatma Gandhi (1869-1948)

God gave us our memories so that we might have roses in December.
James M. Barrie (1860-1937)

That old law about "an eye for an eye" leaves everybody blind. The time is always right to do the right thing.
Rev. Martin Luther King Jr. (1929-68)

This is my simple religion. There is no need for temples; no need for complicated philosophy. Our own brain, our own heart is our temple; the philosophy is kindness.
Dalai Lama (1935-)

When one person suffers from a delusion it is called insanity; when many people suffer from a delusion it is called religion.
Robert Pirsig (1928-)

The glory of Christianity is to conquer by forgiveness.
William Blake (1757-1827)

What can be asserted without evidence can also be dismissed without evidence.
Christopher Hitchens (1949-2011)

Religion ends and philosophy begins, just as alchemy ends and chemistry begins, and astrology ends and astronomy begins.
Richard Dawkins (1941-)

I always distrust people who know so much about what God wants them to do to their fellows.
Susan B Anthony (1820 - 1906)

Just in terms of allocation of time resources, religion is not very efficient. There's a lot more I could be doing on a Sunday morning.
Bill Gates (1955 -)

If I told you to wish for good health, you would think I'm ridiculous; but when I exchange the word "wish" for the word "pray", you believe it can work. That is the disempowering delusion religions have brought us.

Steve Maraboli

Faith is to believe what you do not yet see; the reward for this faith is to see what you believe.

Augustine of Hippo (354 -430)

One and God make a majority.

Frederick Douglas (1818 – 95)

We have just enough religion to make us hate, but not enough to make us love one another.

Jonathan Swift (1667 – 1745)

SCIENCE

The important thing in science is not so much to obtain new facts as to discover new ways of thinking about them.
William Lawrence Bragg (1890-1971)

My mind is my laboratory.
Albert Einstein (1879 - 1955)

Those worlds in space are as countless as all the grains of sand on all the beaches of the earth.
Carl Sagan (1934 – 96)

Observation always involves theory.
Edwin Hubble (1889 - 1953)

The only laws of matter are those that our minds must fabricate and the only laws of mind are fabricated for it by matter.
James Clerk Maxwell (1831 - 79)

Physics is imagination in a strait jacket.
John Moffat (1922 - 2012)

The way to do research is to attack the facts at the point of greatest astonishment.
Celia Green (1935-)

If it disagrees with experiment, it's wrong. And that simple statement is the key to science. It doesn't make a difference how beautiful your guess is, it doesn't matter how smart you are, who made the guess, or what his name is. If it disagrees with experiment, it's wrong. That's all there is to it.
Richard Feynman (1918-88)

A fact is a simple statement that everyone believes. It is innocent, unless found guilty. A hypothesis is a novel suggestion that no one wants to believe. It is guilty, until found effective.
Edward Teller (1908-2003)

In the beginning there was nothing, which exploded.
Terry Pratchett (1948-2015)

I... a universe of atoms, an atom in the universe.
Richard Feynman (1918-88)

No amount of experimentation can ever prove me right; a single experiment can prove me wrong.
Albert Einstein (1879 - 1955)

All exact science is dominated by the idea of approximation.
Bertrand Russell (1872-1970)

Scientists should always state the opinions upon which their facts are based.
Anon

The whole of science is nothing more than a refinement of everyday thinking.
Albert Einstein (1879 - 1955)

We feel that even if all possible scientific questions be answered, the problems of life have still not been touched at all.
Ludwig Wittgenstein (1889 – 1951)

If we knew what it was we were doing, it would not be called research, would it?
Albert Einstein (1879 - 1955)

There's two possible outcomes: if the result confirms the hypothesis, then you've made a discovery. If the result is contrary to the hypothesis, then you've made a discovery.
Enrico Fermi (1901-54)

Science is the knowledge of consequences, and dependence of one fact upon another.
Thomas Hobbes (1588-1679)

If quantum mechanics hasn't profoundly shocked you, you haven't understood it yet.
Niels Bohr (1885-1962)

Discovery is the ability to be puzzled by simple things.
Noam Chomsky (1928 -)

I am among those who think that science has great beauty. A scientist in his laboratory is not only a technician: he is also a child placed before natural phenomena which impress him like a fairy tale.
Marie Curie (1867-1934)

As far as the laws of mathematics refer to reality, they are not certain; and as far as they are certain, they do not refer to reality.
Albert Einstein (1879 - 1955)

Skeptical scrutiny is the means, in both science and religion, by which deep thoughts can be winnowed from deep nonsense.
Carl Sagan (1934-96)

Research is what I'm doing when I don't know what I'm doing.
Wernher Von Braun (1912-77)

A new scientific truth does not triumph by convincing its opponents and making them see the light, but rather because its opponents eventually die, and a new generation grows up that is familiar with it.
Max Planck (1858-1947)

Ignorance more frequently begets confidence than does knowledge: it is those who know little, not those who know much, who so positively assert that this or that problem will never be solved by science.
Charles Darwin (1809-82)

What is now proved was once only imagined.
William Blake (1757-1827)

Science is the great antidote to the poison of enthusiasm and superstition.
Adam Smith (1723-90)

All science is either physics or stamp collecting.
Ernest Rutherford (1871-1937)

The only possible conclusion the social sciences can draw is: some do, some don't.
Ernest Rutherford (1871-1937)

Science has proof without any certainty. Creationists have certainty without any proof.
Ashley Montague (1905-99)

Science is a bit like the joke about the drunk who is looking under a lamppost for a key that he has lost on the other side of the street, because that's where the light is. It has no other choice.
Naom Chomsky (1920 -)

Pure mathematics is, in its way, the poetry of logical ideas.
Albert Einstein (1879 - 1955)

The true logic of this world is in the calculus of probabilities.
James Clerk Maxwell (1831 - 79)

Everything should be made as simple as possible, but not simpler.
Albert Einstein (1879 - 1955)

The only reason for time is so that everything doesn't happen at once.
Albert Einstein (1879 - 1955)

Science is a way of thinking much more than it is a body of knowledge.
Carl Sagan (1934 – 96)

Any sufficiently advanced technology is indistinguishable from magic.
Arthur C. Clarke (1917 – 2008)

The saddest aspect of life right now is that science gathers knowledge faster than society gathers wisdom.
Isaac Asimov (1920 – 72)

SUCCESS

The measure of success is not whether you have a tough problem to deal with, but whether it's the same problem you had last year.
John Foster Dulles (1888-1959)

Every success is the mother of countless others.
Henry Ford (1863 – 1947)

Only he who attempts the absurd is capable of achieving the impossible.
Miguel Unamuno (1864-1936)

The secret of success is to know something no one else knows.
Aristotle Onassis (1906-75)

Successful people ask better questions, and as a result, they get better answers.
Anthony Robbins (1960 -)

How you think when you lose determines how long it will be until you win.
GK Chesterton (1874-1936)

It is not the strongest of the species that survive, nor the most intelligent, but the one most responsive to change.
Charles Darwin (1809-1882)

No victor believes in chance.
Friedrich Nietzsche (1844 – 1900)

Exaggeration, the inseparable companion of greatness.
Voltaire (1694 – 1778)

A pessimist sees the difficulty in every opportunity; an optimist sees the opportunity in every difficulty.
Winston Churchill (1874-1965)

Success is a lousy teacher. It seduces smart people into thinking they can't lose.
Bill Gates (1955-)

The most successful men in the end are those whose success is the result of steady accretion. It is the man who carefully advances step by step, with his mind becoming wider and wider - and progressively better able to grasp any theme or situation.
Alexander Graham Bell (1847-1922)

If you wish to be a success in the world, promise everything, deliver nothing.
Napoleon Bonaparte (1769-1821)

Success is doing ordinary things extraordinarily well.
Jim Rohn (1930-2009)

Seventy percent of success is showing up.
Woody Allen (1935-)

For true success ask yourself four questions; Why? Why not? Why not me? Why not now?
James Allan (1979-)

Success is simple. Do what's right, the right way at the right time.
Arnold H Glasgow (1905-98)

We are what we repeatedly do; excellence, then, is not an act but a habit.
Aristotle (384 BC – 322 BC)

Many of life's failures are people who did not realize how close they were to success when they gave up.
Thomas Edison (1847 – 1931)

Enthusiasm is the yeast that makes your hopes shine to the stars.
Henry Ford (1863 – 1947)

Your attitude, not your aptitude, will determine your altitude.
Zig Ziglar (1928 - 2012)

I will be sufficiently rewarded if when telling it to others you will not claim the discovery as your own, but will say it was mine.
Thales of Miletus (624 BC – 546 BC)

A sign of celebrity is that his name is often worth more than his services.
Daniel J. Boorstin (1914 – 2004)

Most people fail in life because they major in minor things.
Anthony Robbins (1960 -)

If you can meet with Triumph and Disaster
And treat those two impostors just the same.
Rudyard Kipling (1865 - 1936)

The secret of all victory lies in the organization of the non-obvious.
Marcus Aurelius (121 – 180)

TRAVEL

The whole object of travel is not to set foot on foreign land; it is at last to set foot on one's own country as a foreign land.
G. K. Chesterton (1874-1936)

The world is a book, and those who do not travel read only a page.
Augustine of Hippo (354 -430)

People travel for the same reason they collect works of art: because the best people do it.
Aldous Huxley (1894 – 1963)

Not all those who wander are lost.
J.R.R. Tolkien (1892 - 1973)

Travel is fatal to prejudice, bigotry, and narrow-mindedness, and many of our people need it sorely on these accounts. Broad, wholesome, charitable views of men and things cannot be acquired by vegetating in one little corner of the earth all one's lifetime.
Mark Twain (1835 - 1910)

The traveler sees what he sees. The tourist sees what he has come to see.
G.K. Chesterton (1874 - 1936)

There are no foreign lands. It is the traveler only who is foreign.
Robert Louis Stevenson (1850 - 94)

The first condition of understanding a foreign country is to smell it.
Rudyard Kipling (1865 - 1936)

We wander for distraction, but we travel for fulfillment.
Hilaire Belloc (1870 - 1953)

He who has seen one cathedral ten times has seen something; he who has seen ten cathedrals once has seen but little; and he who has spent half an hour in each of a hundred cathedrals has seen nothing at all.
Sinclair Lewis (1885 - 1951)

Truth

There is truth in wine and children.
Plato (428 BC – 348 BC)

Truth is not determined by majority vote.
Doug Gwyn (1948-)

All things are subject to interpretation whichever interpretation prevails at a given time is a function of power and not truth.
Friedrich Nietzsche (1844 – 1900)

I am very fond of truth, but not at all of martyrdom.
Voltaire (1694 – 1778)

Truth is a fruit which should not be plucked until it is ripe.
Voltaire (1694 – 1778)

The victor will never be asked if he told the truth.
Adolf Hitler (1889-1945)

The pursuit of truth and beauty is a sphere of activity in which we are permitted to remain children all our lives.
Albert Einstein (1879 - 1955)

Half a truth is often a great lie.
Benjamin Franklin (1706-90)

Truth is like the sun. You can shut it out for a time, but it ain't goin' away.
Elvis Presley (1935-77)

The opposite of a fact is falsehood, but the opposite of one profound truth may very well be another profound truth.
Niels Bohr (1885-1962)

There are few nudities so objectionable as the naked truth.
Agnes Repplier (1855-1950)

The truth is always a compound of two half-truths, and you never reach it, because there is always something more to say.
Tom Stoppard (1937-)

You can only find truth with logic if you have already found it without it.
GK Chesterton (1874-1936)

Believe those who are seeking the truth. Doubt those who find it.
André Gide (1869-1951)

Whoever is careless with the truth in small matters cannot be trusted with important matters.
Albert Einstein (1879 - 1955)

Most of the change we think we see in life is due to truths being in and out of favor.
Robert Frost (1874 – 1963)

Reality is that which, when you stop believing in it, doesn't go away.
Philip K. Dick (1928 – 82)

Today I bent the truth to be kind, and I have no regret, for I am far surer of what is kind than I am of what is true.
Robert Brault (1963 -)

Men occasionally stumble over the truth, but most of them pick themselves up and hurry off as if nothing ever happened.
Winston Churchill (1874 - 65)

The truth is, of course, that what one regards as interruptions are precisely one's life.
C.S. Lewis (1898 – 1963)

The sea drives truth into a man like salt.
Hilaire Belloc (1870 - 1953)

The great enemy of the truth is very often not the lie -- deliberate, contrived and dishonest, but the myth, persistent, persuasive, and unrealistic. Belief in myths allows the comfort of opinion without the discomfort of thought.
John Fitzgerald Kennedy (1917 – 63)

WAR

War doesn't determine who's right. War determines who's left.
Bertrand Russell (1872-1970)

A single death is a tragedy; a million deaths is a statistic.
Joseph Stalin (1878-1953)

Victory has a thousand fathers, but defeat is an orphan.
John F Kennedy (1917 – 63)

Never interrupt your opponent while he's making a mistake.
Napoleon (1769-1821)

Opinion has caused more trouble on this little earth than plagues or earthquakes.
Voltaire (1694 – 1778)

The best way to destroy an enemy is to make him a friend.

Abraham Lincoln (1809-65)

There is no flag large enough to cover the shame of killing innocent people.
Howard Zinn (1922-2010)

It is only the dead who have seen the end of war.
Plato (428 BC – 348 BC)

In war, there are no unwounded soldiers.
Jose Narosky (1930-)

Once we have a war there is only one thing to do. It must be won. For defeat brings worse things than any that can ever happen in war.
Ernest Hemingway (1899-1961)

It has become appallingly obvious that our technology has exceeded our humanity.
Albert Einstein (1879 - 1955)

War is a poor chisel to carve out tomorrow.
Martin Luther King, Jr. (1929-68)

There is no avoiding war; it can only be postponed to the advantage of others.
Niccolo Machiavelli (1469-1527)

Television brought the brutality of war into the comfort of the living room. Vietnam was lost in the living rooms of America-- not on the battlefields of Vietnam.
Marshall McLuhan (1911 - 80)

The most shocking fact about war is that its victims and its instruments are individual human beings, and that these individual beings are condemned by the monstrous conventions of politics to murder or be murdered in quarrels not their own.
Aldous Huxley (1894-1963)

But in modern war you will die like a dog for no good reason.
Ernest Hemingway (1899-1961)

The choice is not between violence and nonviolence but between nonviolence and nonexistence.
Martin Luther King Jr. (1929-68)

In peace, sons bury their fathers. In war, fathers bury their sons.
Herodotus (484 BC- 425 BC)

War is a severe doctor; but it sometimes heals grievances.
Edward Counsel (1849-1939)

Military glory - that attractive rainbow that rises in showers of blood.
Abraham Lincoln (1809-65)

An eye for an eye only makes the whole world blind.
Mahatma Gandhi (1869-1948)

The dangerous man is the one who has only one idea, because then he'll fight and die for it.
Francis Crick (1916-2004)

In preparing for battle I have always found that plans are useless, but planning is indispensable.
Dwight D. Eisenhower (1890-1969)

I am become death, the destroyer of worlds.
J. Robert Oppenheimer (1904-67)

If I have seen further than others, it is by standing upon the shoulders of giants.
Isaac Newton (1643-1927)

A good plan vigorously executed right now is far better than a perfect plan executed next week.
George S. Patton (1885-1945)

Never ascribe to malice, that which can be explained by incompetence.
Napoleon (1769-1821)

When the rich wage war it's the poor who die.
Jean-Paul Sartre (1905-80)

You may not be interested in war, but war is interested in you.
Leon Trotsky (1879-1940)

Wars are poor chisels for carving out peaceful tomorrows.
Martin Luther King Jr. (1929-68)

Never attempt to win by force what can be won by deception.
Niccolò Machiavelli (1469-1527)

Wars are necessary to teach us lessons we seem unable to learn any other way.
Henry Ford (1863 – 1947)

All war is a symptom of man's failure as a thinking animal.
John Steinbeck (1902 -68)

We all remember how many religious wars were fought for a religion of love and gentleness; how many bodies were burned alive with the genuinely kind intention of saving souls from the eternal fire of hell.
Karl Popper (1902 – 94)

The most effective way to destroy people is to deny and obliterate their own understanding of their history.
George Orwell (1903 -50)

Anyone who has ever looked into the glazed eyes of a soldier dying on the battlefield will think hard before starting a war.
Otto von Bismarck (1815-98)

Rules are for children. This is war, and in war the only crime is to lose.
Joe Abercrombie (1974 -)

No poor bastard ever won a war by dying for his country. He won it by making other bastards die for their country.
General George S. Patton (1885-1945)

The true soldier fights not because he hates what is in front of him, but because he loves what is behind him.
G.K. Chesterton (1874 - 1936)

Only the dead have seen the end of war.
Plato (428 BC – 348 BC)

WISDOM

Wise men speak because they have something to say; fools because they have to say something.
Plato (428 BC – 348 BC)

I hear and I forget. I see and I remember. I do and I understand.
Confucius (551 BC – 479 BC)

I've learned that people will forget what you said, people will forget what you did, but people will never forget how you made them feel.
Maya Angelou (1928-2014)

Wisdom cannot be directly transmitted, and does not readily accumulate through the ages.
Edwin Hubble (1889 - 1953)

Honesty is the first chapter of the book wisdom.
Thomas Jefferson (1743 – 1826)

There is far more opportunity than there is ability.
Thomas Edison (1847 – 1931)

No, that is the great fallacy: the wisdom of old men. They do not grow wise. They grow careful.
Ernest Hemmingway (1899 – 1961)

Science investigates; religion interprets. Science gives man knowledge which is power; religion gives man wisdom which is control.
Martin Luther King (1929 -68)

I have noticed that even people who claim everything is predetermined and that we can do nothing to change it, look before they cross the road.
Stephen Hawking (1942 -)

God, grant me the serenity to accept the things I cannot change, the courage to change the things I can, and the wisdom to know the difference.
Reinhold Niebuhr (1892 – 1971)

The key to wisdom is knowing all the right questions.
John A Simone (1912 – 2000)

By three methods we may learn wisdom: first, by reflection, which is noblest; second, by imitation, which is easiest; and third, by experience, which is the most bitter.
Confucius (551 BC – 479 BC)

It requires wisdom to understand wisdom: The music is nothing if the audience is deaf.
Walter Lippmann (1889 – 1974)

The wisest thing is time, for it brings everything to light.
Thales of Miletus (624 BC – 546 BC)

WOMEN

Curve: The loveliest distance between two points.
Mae West (1893-1980)

Woman's virtue is man's greatest invention.
Cornelia Otis Skinner (1899-1979)

Clever and attractive women do not want to vote; they are willing to let men govern as long as they govern men.
George Bernard Shaw (1856-1950)

Women speak two languages, one of which is verbal.
William Shakespeare (1564-1616)

The silliest woman can manage a clever man; but it needs a very clever woman to manage a fool.
Rudyard Kipling (1865-1936)

You'll lose a lot of money, chasing women. But you'll never lose women, chasing money.
Mario Tomasello (1912-2000)

No woman marries for money; they are all clever enough, before marrying a millionaire, to fall in love with him first.
Cesare Pavese (1908-50)

Every woman is wrong until she cries, and then she is right, instantly.
Thomas C. Haliburton (1796-1865)

I asked a Burmese why women, after centuries of following their men, now walk ahead. He said there were many unexploded land mines since the war.
Robert Mueller (1944-)

In the sex war, thoughtlessness is the weapon of the male, vindictiveness of the female.
Cyril Connolly (1903-74)

Ah, women. They make the highs higher and the lows more frequent.
Friedrich Nietzsche (1844 – 1900)

A lady's imagination is very rapid; it jumps from admiration to love, from love to matrimony in a moment.
Jane Austen (1775-1817)

The great question that has never been answered, and which I have not yet been able to answer, despite my thirty years of research into the feminine soul, is "What does a woman want?"
Sigmund Freud (1856-1939)

There are only two types of women - goddesses and doormats.
Pablo Picasso (1881-1973)

Taught from infancy that beauty is woman's scepter, the mind shapes itself to the body, and roaming round its gilt cage, only seeks to adorn its prison.
Mary Wollstonecraft Shelley (1797-1851)

Women need a reason to have sex. Men just need a place.
Billy Crystal (1948-)

Women who seek to be equal with men lack ambition.
Timothy Leary (1920-96)

A woman's guess is much more accurate than a man's certainty.
Rudyard Kipling (1865 – 1936)

I do not wish them [women] to have power over men; but over themselves.
Mary Wollstonecraft (1759-97)

A wise woman puts a grain of sugar into everything she says to a man, and takes a grain of salt with everything he says to her.
Helen Rowland (1875-1950)

There is one thing more exasperating than a wife who can cook and won't, and that's a wife who can't cook and will.
Robert Frost (1874 – 1963)

A woman is the only thing I am afraid of that I know will not hurt me.
Abraham Lincoln (1809 – 65)

You see a lot of smart guys with dumb women, but you hardly ever see a smart woman with a dumb guy.
Erica Jong (1942 -)

Women should be obscene and not heard.
Groucho Marx (1890 – 1977)

Women have two weapons - cosmetics and tears.
Anon

Plain women know more about men than beautiful ones do. But beautiful women don't need to know about men. It's the men who have to know about beautiful women.
Katherine Hepburn (1907 – 2003)

For most of history, Anonymous was a woman.
Virginia Woolf (1882 – 1941)

There are no good girls gone wrong - just bad girls found out.
Mae West (1893 – 1980)

Women and cats will do as they please, and men and dogs should relax and get used to the idea.
Robert A. Heinlein (1907 – 88)

WORK

Every employee rises to the level of his own incompetence.
Laurence J. Peter (1919-90)

Of course I don't look busy, I did it right the first time.
Scotts Adams (1957-)

Find out what you like doing best and get someone to pay you for doing it.
Katherine Whitehorn (1928-)

What gets measured gets managed.
Peter Drucker (1909-2005)

Whoever best describes a problem is the one most likely to solve it.
Dan Roam

Management is doing things right; leadership is doing the right things.
Peter Drucker (1909-2005)

Dreams don't work unless you do.
John C. Maxwell (1947-)

I'm a great believer in luck, and I find the harder I work the more I have of it.
Thomas Jefferson (1743-1826)

Basically, I no longer work for anything but the sensation I have while working.
Albert Giacometti (1901-66)

Whoever controls work and wages, controls morals.
Susan B Anthony (1820 -1906)

Work is more fun than fun.
Noël Coward (1899 – 1973)

Work is the refuge of people who have nothing better to do.
Oscar Wilde (1854 - 1900)

Work spares us from three evils: boredom, vice, and need.
Voltaire (1694 - 1778)

ONE LAST THING…

If you enjoyed this book or found it useful I'd be very grateful if you'd post a short review on Amazon. Your support really does make a difference and I read all the reviews personally so I can get your feedback and make this book even better.

If you'd like to leave a review, then all you need to do is click the review link on this book's Amazon page.

M. Prefontaine

Printed in Dunstable, United Kingdom